THE DANIEL DILEMMA

REAL COURAGE FOR REAL LIFE
RAND HUMMEL

journey**forth**®

Greenville, South Carolina

Library of Congress Cataloging-in Publication Data
Names: Hummel, Rand, 1956- author.
Title: The Daniel dilemma : real courage for real life / Rand Hummel.
Description: Greenville : JourneyForth, 2016. | Includes bibliographical
references. | Description based on print version record and CIP data
provided by publisher; resource not viewed.
Identifiers: LCCN 2015048650 (print) | LCCN 2015046792 (ebook) | ISBN
9781628562200 (ebook) | ISBN 9781628562194 (perfect bound pbk. : alk.
paper)
Subjects: LCSH: Bible. Daniel—Criticism, interpretation, etc. | Christian
Teenagers—Religious life. | Christian teenagers—Conduct of life.
Classification: LCC BS1555.52 (print) | LCC BS1555.52 .H86 2016 (ebook) | DDC
248.8/3—dc23
LC record available at http://lccn.loc.gov/2015048650

Art Director: Elly Kalagayan
Designer: NaEun Hyun
Page layout: Michael Boone

Dedicated to Sebi
(Sebastian Rand Hummel)

I trust that you will grow up
to be a lion-like leader
just like your dad.

CONTENTS

INTRODUCTION

Lions are not on the official endangered species list, but *lion-like leaders* are really close.

As the king of the beasts, the lion is the largest and strongest member of the cat family and has no natural enemies. Even elephants and water buffaloes are not looking to the lions for their next meal. Lions are listed as "vulnerable" by the IUCN (*International Union for the Conservation of Nature*)[1]—one rung below an official endangered listing. Lion kings are in decline. There are an estimated 30,000 lions remaining in all of Africa down from perhaps 200,000 in the 1970s.

Species and ecosystems are designated with either an *X* (*presumed extinct*) if there is no expectation that they still survive, or an *H* (*possibly extinct*) if they are known only from historical records but there is a chance they may still exist.[2]

Most conservationists rank the estimated extinction risk of plants and animals on a one-to-five scale, ranging from *1* (*critically imperiled*) to *5* (*secure*).

1 = critically imperiled

2 = imperiled

3 = vulnerable

4 = apparently secure

5 = secure

Strong spiritual leaders among teens in youth groups, churches, high schools, colleges, and ministries can neither be *X* (*presumed extinct*) or considered *H* (*possibly extinct*) although such leadership potential is far from 5 (*secure*), and if not 2 (*imperiled*), it is certainly 3 (*vulnerable*). How many strong, spiritual leaders do *you* have to look up to? Are you the kind of leader other teens desire to follow? We need more Daniels and Danielles.

The importance of character, integrity, and spiritual courage cannot be overestimated. There are not enough blocks and filters to protect us from the onslaught of our media world. There are not enough retreats, private schools, or care groups to isolate us from the antagonism of a godless world. There are not enough counselors or programs to enable us to escape from the intense passions and lusts of our own flesh. What you need is the kind of divinely enabled character that Daniel had if you are to become the future lion-like leaders of your world.

How did Daniel do it? From age 15 to age 85 he refused to be assimilated into or blended with the world he was forced to live in. His life was threatened by egotistical Nebuchadnezzar, mocked by wicked Belshazzar, and sentenced to death in a lions' den by King Darius. Through all of this he never lost his integrity. Daniel was a man of lion-like character, and everyone knew it.

King Darius preferred Daniel over all his other leadership team because of the "excellent spirit" (Daniel 5:12) that Daniel possessed. Here is a true picture of divinely enabled leadership, for such a superior, excellent spirit comes only from God. Although he was not a superhero, he did possess supernatural power. He was supernaturally controlled by God's amazing, excellent, and enabling grace.

The dynamic tension between what God commands you to do and what you depend on God to do for you is a very interesting study. True lion-like character—character that lasts—combines our efforts with God's enablement. You must work like it all depends on you and trust like it all depends on God! It is not an *either-or* proposition but a *both-and* way of life. Paul said, "I also labor, striving according to His working which works in me mightily" (Colossians 1:29 NKJV) and "I labored more abundantly than they all: yet not I, but the grace of God which was with me" (1 Corinthians 15:10). The Israelites experienced this as they were told to step into the Jordan; the widow of Zarephath saw this truth after she made a cake for Elijah; James wrestled with this as he dealt with faith and works in his letter, and you experience it each time you exercise your mustard-seed-sized faith and watch God make it grow. Solomon wisely counsels us to remember that "the horse is prepared against the day of battle [prepared by man]: but safety is of the Lord" (Proverbs 21:31.)

The importance of character, integrity, and spiritual courage cannot be overestimated. Daniel lived a life with lion-like character, and so can you. Enjoy your study and remember that Daniel could have never faced the lions with confidence if he had not met God face-to-face three times a day.

Rand Hummel

PART ONE

LIVING WITH LION-LIKE INTEGRITY

Daniel did it and so can you!

A MEDITATION ON DANIEL 6:1–28

I think you've all seen enough flannelgraph stories to know what the prophet-statesman Daniel looked like (a lot like Jacob the week before and Abraham the week before that). But how much do you really know about this remarkable man?

If during the millennial reign I have the opportunity to spend some time with men and women that lived hundreds of years before me, I want to sit in the same coffee shop with Daniel and listen to the questions he is asked. I assume that most of us would ask Daniel about what it was like in the lions' den—"Were you scared? How many lions were there? Did they get close enough to see their teeth? Smell their breath? Did you use one for a pillow as you slept that night?" Sad to say, most of us would be more interested in his lions' den experience than his upper room prayer habits.

You would do well to meditate on Daniel 6:1–28 and try to catch the serious drama that Daniel, well-seasoned in character and integrity, faced after living for over seventy years in a culture hostile to his God. That culture was not unlike what you and your families face in your world today.

DANIEL 6:1–2

It pleased Darius to set over the kingdom an hundred and twenty princes, which should be over the whole kingdom; and over these three presidents; of whom Daniel was first: that the princes might give accounts unto them, and the king should have no damage.

After the Persian conquest of Babylon, King Darius the Mede ruled the city and organized his government with obvious checks and balances by placing the entire population under 120 princes who were accountable to three presidents, of whom Daniel was first in charge.

Daniel was outnumbered 122 to 1. He was a roadblock to the riches and ease that a government (tax-funded) lifestyle could afford. With Daniel around, there were no special favors, no special interest groups, and no private funding under the table.

Accountability is essential, even in a pagan world. The princes were accountable to the presidents who were accountable to Daniel who was accountable to Darius who (whether he knew it or not) was accountable to God.

DANIEL 6:3–5

Then this Daniel was preferred [distinguished] above the presidents and princes, because an excellent spirit was in him; and the king thought to set him over the whole realm [the entire kingdom]. Then the presidents and princes sought to find occasion [grounds for complaint] against Daniel concerning the kingdom; but they could find none occasion nor fault; forasmuch as he was faithful, neither was there any error or fault found in him. Then said these men, We shall not find any occasion against this Daniel, except we find it against him concerning the law of his God.

Daniel Was Preferred . . .

Why did King Darius *prefer* Daniel over the others? What caused Daniel to distinguish himself above the other leaders? It was not his youthful enthusiasm at this time, he was over eighty! It was not his popularity. Daniel was ganged up on—122 against 1—but even with such odds, King Darius preferred the 1 over the 122. It was nothing external—looks, wealth, political ties, celebrity status. Darius was impressed with Daniel's "excellent spirit."

An Excellent Spirit Was in Him . . .

Daniel had a spirit, an attitude, a way about him, that as he did his work and mingled with his co-workers, surpassed the spirits and attitudes of all those around him. He was not moody. He could not be accused of being lazy. He obviously was not spacey or forgetful. He was different from those around him. All were leaders with influence and intelligence. But Daniel possessed something that the others lacked. Here is a true picture of divinely enabled leadership, for such a superior, excellent spirit comes only from God. Although Daniel was not a superhero, he did possess a supernatural power. He was supernaturally controlled by God's amazing (excellent) grace! God gives grace only to the humble—those who put Him and others before themselves as did Daniel for his eighty-plus years. The 122 were proud, envious men; God's grace cannot coexist with envy.

There are many common negative characteristics that have become epidemic in our godless world.

- Pride says, "I am now the leader, look at me!"
- Selfishness insists, "I'm in charge. I'll do it my way."
- Greed declares, "I love the perks of leadership, no matter what it costs others."
- Laziness gripes, "That's not my job. Who do you think I am?"

- Ingratitude complains, "I have earned what I have and probably deserve more."

And the King Thought to Set Him over the Whole Realm . . .

Daniel was being considered to serve as the CEO of Babylon and all its provinces. Seventy years earlier he refused to eat the king's meat and now he would have the authority to decide what kind of meat the king would eat. When you add the characteristics of *excellence* to *faithfulness*, you get a leader with lion-like character. Daniel filled his trust account with respect. Such honor and opportunity is purchased with the high cost of faithfulness.

Daniel illustrated a New Testament principle our Lord Jesus Christ shared a number of times with His followers regarding faithfulness.

> His lord said unto him, Well done, thou good and faithful servant: thou hast been faithful over a few things, I will make thee ruler over many things: enter thou into the joy of thy lord. (Matthew 25:21)

> He that is faithful in that which is least is faithful also in much: and he that is unjust in the least is unjust also in much. (Luke 16:10)

> And He said unto him, Well, thou good servant: because thou hast been faithful in a very little, have thou authority over ten cities. (Luke 19:17)

They Could Find None Occasion Nor Fault . . .

The governors of more than one hundred provinces gathered secretly to set in motion a plan to discredit Daniel in the eyes of King Darius. With him around, their plans for self-exaltation would never succeed. Discredit? He was not a drunk. He was not a womanizer. He did not show favoritism to any special interest groups. His finances were squeaky clean.

If Daniel would just join in with them, Daniel could have what they hoped to have by ripping off the king's loyal subjects—possibly expensive chariots, elegant vacation packages at Persian resorts, luxurious apartments, and the finest cuisine that stolen and misappropriated taxes could afford.

None Occasion . . .

There was no occasion when he did not do his job; no occasion or grounds of accusation for taking anything from work—not even a Babylonian paper clip; no occasion or opportunity of complaint for the long hours demanded by his position; no occasion of complaining about his superior; no occasion where he got upset with his coworkers because of their lack of diligence or discipline. No occasion; nothing!

No Fault . . .

There was no evidence of corruption; nothing wrong with the way he administered the kingdom; no blame; no malice; no blunder; no mistake; no slipup; no oversight; no lapse in judgment; no crack in his character; no unreconciled relationship; no harsh words. Nothing!

He Was Faithful . . .

He did not come in late to work. He refused to waste company time talking about the latest races. He did his job and did it well, so well that even King Darius saw the difference, and he liked what he saw. Faithfulness goes a long way in the eyes of both believers and unbelievers. You could trust Daniel. If you needed a friend, he was the one to go to. You could always count on him. Unexpected sacrifice was a way of life for Daniel. He fulfilled what he consented to do and did it with an excellent spirit. He was faithful.

Except We Find It against Him Concerning the Law of His God . . .

Daniel's work ethic and moral integrity were impeccable. What made him different (and most don't like *different*) were his open religious views and his fanatical commitment to his God. His relationship with the living God put a bull's-eye on the back of his toga for the liberal-minded atheistic world to take aim. We can only speculate on what the 122 would say at their get-togethers—the ones that Daniel was not invited to attend.

- "He won't worship *our* Babylonian deities."
- "He won't even acknowledge Bel, Marduch or Bel-Merodach."
- "He prays to *his* God three times a day!"
- "He thinks his holy writings are directly from his God."
- "He thinks he is better than us and won't even eat what we eat!"
- "He touts that his God is the only *living* God!"

Then these presidents and princes assembled together to the king, and said thus unto him, King Darius, live for ever. All [Lie! All but Daniel] the presidents of the kingdom, the governors, and the princes, the counsellors, and the captains, have consulted together to establish a royal statute, and to make a firm decree, that whosoever shall ask a petition of any God or man for thirty days, save of thee, O king, he shall be cast into the den of lions. Now, O king, establish the decree, and sign the writing, that it be not changed, according to the law of the Medes and Persians, which altereth not. Wherefore king Darius signed the writing and the decree. (Daniel 6:6–9)

King Darius had to be lied to in order to make such a decree. He already showed his respect for Daniel and, without thinking, assumed Daniel was part of this request. The king was wrong.

King Darius had to be tricked into making their suggestion a royal law because they knew that once the king realized that this law was Daniel's death sentence, he would reverse the order. Now he could not. He signed a document that made Daniel's faith illegal and unknowingly put himself in the place of God.

King Darius violated King Solomon's inspired advice, "He who answers a matter before he hears it, it is folly and shame to him" (Proverbs 18:13 NKJV), as he signed the statute before studying it. How often you act before you think and regret it later.

The king pleased the crowd by signing the decree and *later regretted it*.

The presidents, princes, governors, counselors, and captains were pleased with themselves as they choreographed Daniel's death and *later regretted it*.

Daniel pleased his God as he faced a life-and-death dilemma from his eighty-year-old knees and *never regretted it*.

DANIEL 6:10

Now when Daniel knew that the writing was signed, he went into his house; and his windows being open in his chamber toward Jerusalem, he kneeled upon his knees three times a day, and prayed, and gave thanks before his God, as he did aforetime.

When Daniel Knew That the Writing Was Signed, He Went into His House and Prayed . . .

Daniel went to his prayer chamber and prayed even in the face of a lions' den. If that same decree were given this month, would you still go to prayer meeting? The attendance at prayer meeting is meager at best without the threat of lions. Can you imagine the impact of such a decree in most of our Bible-believing churches?

Since there are no lions' dens to scare you into silence before God, why are you so silent? What if you had to pay for the privilege of praying, say $89 a month for unlimited access to God? Would you be willing to take on the monthly cost? Would you take as much advantage in communicating with God as you do with your cell phone plan? Would you ever be charged with excessive texts or going over your allotment of minutes with God?

What *would* it take to make you stop praying for thirty days? A thousand dollars? A new iPad? A better job? A promise of a life partner? A spot on the team? A new house? A shot at world recognition or fame? What?

What *does* it take to keep you from praying consistently for thirty days? Apathy? Laziness? A shallow relationship with Jesus Christ? Friends? Facebook? Video games? What?

If a den of lions causes you to give up your privilege of talking to God, what is next? If you are so quick and willing to give up your prayer life, is your thought life next? Your personal integrity? Your personal purity? Your obedience to God's Word? Your trust in God and God alone?

His Windows Being Open in His Chamber toward Jerusalem . . .

What was the big deal of Daniel's windows being open? Can't God hear you through the walls? Aren't you supposed to hide in your closet with the door closed and pray? Daniel's windows were not open for a show to reveal how much more spiritual he was than others. They were open as one small way to praise Jehovah God in a pagan culture—one small way to show how important his holy God was to him in a hostile world.

Many would say, "I, too, would march right up to that prayer chamber and with windows wide open pray to God!" Really? Do you keep the windows open in your school cafeteria? Do you keep the windows open at McDonald's, Olive Garden, or Pizza Hut? Do you keep the windows open in church by bowing your head and involving yourself in corporate prayer? Way too many shut the windows of prayer to God and the windows of blessing from God.

Oh, for the courageous heart of Daniel. The simple things that identified him with the cause of Jehovah God he held to tightly. If I were a Marine, I would proudly wear the uniform of a Marine; if I joined the Army, I would be honored to march in my parade blues; I would not hide the fact that I was a soldier! But to hide the fact that you are a Christian seems to be quite acceptable—look like an unbeliever, talk like an unbeliever, live like an unbeliever. Go ahead and shut the windows so no one sees you talk to God.

He Kneeled . . .

What humility, even in his eighties. The position of our praying can often express the condition of our hearts. You don't have to kneel, but it does not hurt to kneel. If you cannot concentrate while seated or standing, kneel. You should never kneel to be seen by others, but for our hearts to be seen by God.

Throughout Scripture, enthusiastic thanksgiving to God is often expressed with hands lifted up to God; when hearts are overwhelmed with sorrow, many fall to their knees or even to the ground with faces buried in their hands with no compulsion to open their eyes or even look towards heaven. Sometimes you want to weep, and other times you want to shout. At times your heart desires to quietly thank God for His goodness, and other times you want to clap your hands for joy. There is no mandate, no box, only the uninhibited expression of delight in what God has done for us. Why are you hesitant to worship the way your heart desires? You do have to be careful not to draw undue attention to yourself, and any extremes in corporate worship could draw attention and distract others from their focus on the Lord. So in public, you need to be careful and think of those around you. But, if it is just you and God, go for it!

Lift up your hands in the sanctuary, and bless the Lord. (Psalm 134:2)

O come, let us worship and bow down: let us kneel before the Lord our Maker. (Psalm 95:6)

And he was withdrawn from them about a stone's cast, and kneeled down, and prayed. (Luke 22:41)

For this cause I bow my knees unto the Father of our Lord Jesus Christ. (Ephesians 3:14)

And he went forward a little, and fell on the ground, and prayed that, if it were possible, the hour might pass from him. (Mark 14:35)

And he leaping up stood, and walked, and entered with them into the temple, walking, and leaping, and praising God. (Acts 3:8)

I will lift up mine eyes unto the hills, from whence cometh my help. (Psalm 121:1)

O clap your hands, all ye people; shout unto God with the voice of triumph. (Psalm 47:1)

Three Times a Day . . .

Although Daniel was a busy man as the prime minister of the Medo-Persian Empire, he kept his schedule clear for prayer. It was not an add-on, but a part of his interwoven character.

Combine a contrite heart with a consistent walk, and you will find someone on their knees before God three times a day. Anything consistently done *three times a day*, can and will become a habit. There is much to be said about breaking *bad* habits, but you should emphasize the necessity of building *good* habits. "Three times a day" could be another way of saying, "morning, noon, and night." What kind of change do you think you would see in your walk with God if you followed David's practice?

Evening, and morning, and at noon, will I pray, and cry aloud: and he shall hear my voice. (Psalm 55:17)

I prevented the dawning of the morning, and cried: I hoped in thy word. Mine eyes prevent the night watches, that I might meditate in thy word. (Psalm 119:147–148)

And Prayed, and Gave Thanks before His God, As He Did Aforetime ...

To lead others closer to God, a leader must know how to talk to God.

Men ought always to pray, and not to faint (Luke 18:1)

E. M. Bounds wrote that "the goal of prayer is the ear of God."[1]

The effectual fervent prayer of a righteous man availeth much. (James 5:16)

Even though prayer is a lonely business, you are never truly alone.

Corrie Ten Boom said that "faith sees the invisible, believes the unbelievable and receives the impossible."[2]

Prayer is not gritting your teeth, but falling in love. Not even a den of hungry lions could deter Daniel from praying. We all need to thank God more than we do. The best biblical way to send a prayerful thank-you note to God is found in Ephesians 5:20.

Giving thanks always for all things unto God and the Father in the name of our Lord Jesus Christ.

giving—continuous and repeated action

always—at all times; perpetual; over and over; continuous; forever

for all things—the total package, not just the parts you like but the entirety

unto God and the Father—to God, the heavenly Father; Thanksgiving must have a recipient—the one that has done something that generates a thankful heart. Meditate on God as your loving, heavenly Father, and you will have more to be thankful for than you have minutes in a day.

In the name of our Lord Jesus Christ—through Jesus Christ come all the blessings of eternal life and the benefits of abundant life and what He has done for us; All thanksgiving should return through Him in prayer.

One of Daniel's prayers is recorded for us in Daniel 9:17 where he prays in part, "Cause thy face to shine upon thy sanctuary."

Daniel knew how to keep his focus off himself and to direct it to God and others. Other than Daniel's purposeful character, his faithfulness to his convictions, and his consistency and fervency in prayer, it was his concern for God's people—others—that motivated this octogenarian to live the holy and happy life that he lived. Daniel's prayer was free from selfishness; he didn't pray just for himself. And Daniel's prayer was focused on God.

DANIEL'S PRAYER

Then I set my face toward the Lord God to make request by prayer and supplications, with fasting, sackcloth, and ashes. And I prayed to the Lord my God, and made confession, and said, "O Lord, great and awesome God, who keeps His covenant and mercy with those who love Him, and with those who keep His commandments, we have sinned and committed iniquity, we have done wickedly and rebelled, even by departing from Your precepts and Your judgments. Neither have we heeded Your servants the prophets, who spoke in Your name to our kings and our princes, to our fathers and all the people of the land. O Lord, righteousness belongs to You, but to us shame of face, as it is this day—to the men of Judah, to the inhabitants of Jerusalem and all Israel, those near and those far off in all the countries to which You have driven them, because of the unfaithfulness which they have committed against You.

"O Lord, to us belongs shame of face, to our kings, our princes, and our fathers, because we have sinned against You. To the Lord our God belong mercy and forgiveness, though we have rebelled against Him. We have not obeyed the voice of the Lord our God, to walk in His laws, which

He set before us by His servants the prophets. Yes, all Israel has transgressed Your law, and has departed so as not to obey Your voice; therefore the curse and the oath written in the Law of Moses the servant of God have been poured out on us, because we have sinned against Him. And He has confirmed His words, which He spoke against us and against our judges who judged us, by bringing upon us a great disaster; for under the whole heaven such has never been done as what has been done to Jerusalem.

"As it is written in the Law of Moses, all this disaster has come upon us; yet we have not made our prayer before the Lord our God, that we might turn from our iniquities and understand Your truth. Therefore the Lord has kept the disaster in mind, and brought it upon us; for the Lord our God is righteous in all the works which He does, though we have not obeyed His voice. And now, O Lord our God, who brought Your people out of the land of Egypt with a mighty hand, and made Yourself a name, as it is this day—we have sinned, we have done wickedly!

"O Lord, according to all Your righteousness, I pray, let Your anger and Your fury be turned away from Your city Jerusalem, Your holy mountain; because for our sins, and for the iniquities of our fathers, Jerusalem and Your people are a reproach to all those around us. Now therefore, our God, hear the prayer of Your servant, and his supplications, and for the Lord's sake cause Your face to shine on Your sanctuary, which is desolate. O my God, incline Your ear and hear; open Your eyes and see our desolations, and the city which is called by Your name; for we do not present our supplications before You because of our righteous deeds, but because of Your great mercies. O Lord, hear! O Lord, forgive! O Lord, listen and act! Do not delay for Your own sake, my God, for Your city and Your people are called by Your name." (Daniel 9:3–19 NKJV)

His prayer was from a humble heart. Sackcloth, fasting, and ashes only began to show the true spirit of this aged prayer warrior. His prayer was full of Scripture, much of which was from the old manuscript that Jeremiah wrote and, we assume, Daniel read, meditated on, wept over, and studied. His prayer was filled with excitement and zeal for God's glory.

His prayer was earnest as seen in the repetition of the phrase "O Lord." Maybe he did not sense closeness to God and prayed "O Lord." Maybe his own heart was being overcome with unworthiness as he cried "O Lord." This was not vain repetition, but a thoughtful, needful, crying out to God for recognition of His presence. He pled the covenant reminding God of His promise to Abraham and his people.

God loves to be believed in—"God, you said it, now please do it!" Daniel prayed for the impossible. Jerusalem was in ruins; Judah's sin was excessive; God's people were scattered and enslaved, but God was in control of both kings and kingdoms.

Don't just pray for God's blessings, but for the very presence of God. You shouldn't want God's Spirit simply to be with you, but you should want the Holy Spirit to be glad to be with you, comfortable being with you, and eager to do His work in your life.

DANIEL 6:11-13

Then these men assembled, and found Daniel praying and making supplication before his God. Then they came near, and spake before the king concerning the king's decree; Hast thou not signed a decree, that every man that shall ask a petition of any God or man within thirty days, save of thee, O king, shall be cast into the den of lions? The king answered and said, The thing is true, according to the law of the Medes and Persians, which altereth not. Then answered they and said before the king, That Daniel, which is of the children of the captivity of Judah, regardeth not thee, O king, nor the decree that thou hast signed, but maketh his petition three times a day.

That Daniel . . .

Daniel, do you hear what the men are saying? *"That Daniel." "That Hebrew!" "That believer in Jehovah!"* "Not Belteshazzar, no nickname, but his Hebrew name!"

Which Is of the Children of the Captivity of Judah . . .

"Remember, he is a captive slave! He is nothing! He is a Jew! How low can you get? Wrong race! Got it?"

Regardeth Not Thee, O King . . .

"He doesn't care about you. He pays no attention to you. He is ignoring you and your laws. Daniel has no respect for you and actually looks down on you!"

But Maketh His Petition Three Times a Day . . .

"He still prays to his God three times a day. Our little Sunday school boy needs his crutch to lean on. He is not one of us, doesn't live like us, and doesn't worship like us! Daniel, with his open-window praying makes us very uncomfortable!"

DANIEL 6:14-17

Then the king, when he heard these words, was sore displeased with himself, and set his heart on Daniel to deliver him: and he labored till the going down of the sun to deliver him. Then these men assembled unto the king, and said unto the king, Know, O king, that the law of the Medes and Persians is, That no decree nor statute which the king establisheth may be changed. Then the king commanded, and they brought Daniel, and cast him into the den of lions.

Never think righteous living will keep you out of the lions' dens.

Now the king spake and said unto Daniel, Thy God whom thou servest continually, he will deliver thee. And a stone was brought, and laid upon the mouth of the den; and the king sealed it with his own signet, and with the signet of his lords; that the purpose might not be changed concerning Daniel.

Darius was displeased with himself and did all he could to correct his mistake.

Cast Him into the Den of Lions . . .

Just as Daniel's three friends knew that God would rescue them from the intense flames by deliverance or death, so Daniel knew he would be delivered by God—*from* the lions' mouths or *through* the lions' mouths, *into* their stomachs, and straight on to heaven. No matter which way, he would be rescued by God.

Don't think that by doing right with the right heart motivation you will be kept *from* the lions' dens. Daniel was dropped into such a den. I can't imagine an angry, hissing house cat jumping on my lap let along being dropped into a stone execution chamber wondering how long it would take for the hungry lions to devour me. Daniel was not singled out and attacked because he was unfaithful, but because he *was* faithful! David cried a few years earlier, "Help, Lord; for the godly man ceaseth; for the faithful fail from among the children of men" (Psalm 12:1).

Can you hear the king?

Thy God Whom Thou Servest Continually, He Will Deliver Thee . . .

"Daniel, I've tried everything I could do as king! You don't deserve this. But I know from watching you that if your God is who you say He is, He can deliver you from these lions. I don't know how. But I can hope, fast, and pray that He does."

DANIEL 6:18-20

Then the king went to his palace, and **passed the night fasting**: neither were instruments of musick brought before him: and his sleep went from him. Then the king arose very early in the morning, and went in haste unto the den of lions. And when he came to the den, he cried with a lamentable voice unto Daniel: and the king spake and said to Daniel, O Daniel, servant of the living God, is thy God, whom thou servest continually, able to deliver thee from the lions?

No food; no sleep; no entertainment; no distractions—just fasting and praying! Darius spent a sleepless night, but it sounds like Daniel rested well. Compared to Darius's sleepless night, Daniel spent a splendid night with quiet lions and host of angelic lion tamers. Now that was a night to remember. The king wanted to know. Had God answered his prayers and honored his fasting? Talk about anticipation!

- He arose very early.
- He went in haste.
- He cried with a lamentable voice.
- He was overcome by Daniel's servant's heart and spirit.
- He acknowledged that Daniel's God was a living God.
- He asked if Daniel's God was a miracle-working God.

DANIEL 6:21–23

Then said Daniel unto the king, O king, live for ever. My God hath sent His angel, and hath shut the lions' mouths, that they have not hurt me: forasmuch as before Him innocency was found in me; and also before thee, O king, have I done no hurt. Then was the king exceeding glad for him, and commanded that they should take Daniel up out of the den. So Daniel was taken up out of the den, and no manner of hurt was found upon him, because he believed in his God.

Don't give up or give in. Your antagonizers want their way, but why can't you have yours? If you give in, plan on giving in forever. If you refuse to yield, be willing to be thrown to the lions, but never forget that God is the one that controls the lions' appetites, and your antagonizing friends may look much tastier to them than you.

Remember, Daniel could not have faced the lions with confidence if he had not met face to face with God many times before his open windows. I like what Spurgeon said about Daniel 6:10.

> This showed that he made a business of prayer, and finding it neither convenient to his circumstances nor congenial to his mind to pray in the midst of idolaters, he had chosen to set apart a chamber in his own house for prayer. I don't know how you find it, but there are some of us who never pray so well as by the old arm-chair and in that very room where many a time we have told the Lord our grief, and have poured out before him our transgressions. It is well to have, if we can have, a little room, no matter how humble, where we can shut the door, and pray to our Father who is in heaven, who will hear and answer.[3]

DANIEL 6:24

And the king commanded, and they brought those men which had accused Daniel, and they cast them into the den of lions, them, their children, and their wives; and the lions had the mastery of them, and brake all their bones in pieces or ever they came at the bottom of the den.

This judgment is extreme. This kind of judgment is final. These political liars will never lie again, but sad to say, neither will any members of their families. This proves who has angel protection and who does not. This demonstrated that the lions did not lack hunger when Daniel was thrown in (although all they would have gotten was grit and gristle), but were providentially hindered for a time.

How many were thrown into the den? We don't know. It could have been all 120 princes. Add their families, and it could have easily been over 500 individuals thrown to the lions. As harsh as this seems, it looks like God reversed their deceptive curse, and they suffered the very torture they suggested for Daniel. The end result was that those who refused to pray, refused to cry out to the living God, and refused to petition or ask Him for His leading and protection, were the very ones thrown into the lions' den. Remember, as a leader, when you walk away from God, many will follow—many that you love.

DANIEL 6:25–28

Then king Darius wrote unto all people, nations, and languages, that dwell in all the earth; Peace be multiplied unto you. I make a decree, That in every dominion of my kingdom men tremble and fear before the God of Daniel: for he is the living God, and steadfast for ever, and his kingdom [is the one] that which shall not be destroyed, and His dominion shall be even unto the end. He delivereth and rescueth, and He worketh signs and wonders in heaven and in earth, who hath delivered Daniel from the power of the lions. So this Daniel prospered in the reign of Darius, and in the reign of Cyrus the Persian.

How do you like your windows? Open or shut?

PART TWO

GUARDING AGAINST EXTINCTION

Daniel Principles

WITHSTAND BRAINWASHING TECHNIQUES

Daniel 1:1–8; 2:5, 12–15

Kidnapped? Yes. Brainwashed? No!

When you think about the book of Daniel, normally three pictures come to mind:

1. A burning fiery furnace with four men walking around in the midst of the flames—unharmed

2. Nebuchadnezzar's tall statue made of gold, silver, bronze, iron, and clay

3. Daniel, sound asleep, with his head resting on a lioness with two lion cubs cuddling up to him

There is a much bigger picture often unnoticed—that is of four teenaged POWs, survivors of a military siege, kidnapped and taken to Babylon. There, King Nebuchadnezzar began his brainwashing endeavors on these intelligent, good-looking, and gifted young men (much like those of you reading this book). His goal was not to annihilate them (destroy them) but to assimilate them (blend them in) by getting *Jerusalem* (the city of God) out of them and putting *Babylon* (the center of worldly culture) into them. If he could just get them, in a short amount of time, to *think* like a Babylonian, he would succeed. He used well-proven, brainwashing techniques: (1) isolation, (2) indoctrination, (3) identification, and (4) intimidation to do so. Commentator Sinclair Ferguson put it this way.

> The way we **think**—about God, ourselves, others, the world—determines the way we **live**. If Nebuchadnezzar could only get these men to **think** like Babylonians, then they would *live* like Babylonians. Conversely, so long as they **thought** of themselves as the Lord's, they would *live* as His servants—even in Babylon. That principle is still true. The secret of faithfully living for God today lies in the way we **think**. We are not to be conformed to the world [brainwashed], says Paul. Yet how can we avoid it? Christians have their lives transformed by the renewing of their minds.[1] (author's emphasis in bold)

Ready to dig in? Let's start our journey with Daniel, Hananiah, Mishael, and Azariah, but don't be surprised if this adventure gets a bit uncomfortable—even convicting— at times. These were four normal teen guys that loved God but were forced to live way outside of their comfort zone as prisoners of war.

> In the third year of the reign of Jehoiakim king of Judah came Nebuchadnezzar king of **Babylon** unto **Jerusalem**, and **besieged** it. And the Lord gave Jehoiakim king of Judah into his hand, with part of the vessels of the house of God: which he carried into the land of Shinar to the house of his god; and he brought the vessels into the treasure house of his god. (Daniel 1:1–2)

The book of Daniel is a story of the struggle between the culture of the world and the culture of God. Babylon's culture is a proud display of what man blindly thinks he accomplishes without God. The city of Babylon has massive walls and a huge moat—no need for God's protection. The commerce of Babylon had incredible wealth with its hanging gardens, golden statues, and Ishtar Gate—no need for God's provision. The people of Babylon had their own home-made gods—Bel, Marduch, Bel-Merodach—that gave them what they wanted without any accountability—no need for God. God allowed the Babylonian world to have what they wanted—life without Him—which they are still experiencing in their eternal state as you read this book. Right now, those same Babylonians of Daniel's day would give a thousand Babylons for just one day in heaven before the presence of God. No one can accuse God of being unfair. He often gives men just what they live for, just what they desire, and just what they think they want—life without Him.

Brainwashing Techniques

In the late 1950s, psychologist Robert Jay Lifton studied former prisoners of the Korean and Chinese war camps. He determined that they'd undergone a multistep process that began with attacks on the prisoner's sense of self and ended with what appeared to be a change in beliefs. Each of these stages takes place in an environment of isolation, meaning all *normal* social reference points are unavailable, replaced with mind-clouding techniques like sleep deprivation and malnutrition and the constant threat of physical harm. Lifton identified three stages: (1) breaking down the self, (2) introducing the possibility of escape or salvation, and (3) rebuilding the self.[2]

Satan seeks to do the same to us. If he can control our minds, he can control our lives. Here is his own toolbox of brainwashing techniques.

- Isolation—living without any godly influence
- Indoctrination—learning to be comfortable with the world
- Identification—losing your unique identification with Christ

- Intimidation—letting fear, peer pressure, and unrealistic threats control you

And the king spake unto Ashpenaz the master of his eunuchs, that he should bring certain of the children of Israel, and of the king's seed, and of the princes; children in whom was no blemish, but well favored, and skillful in all wisdom, and cunning in knowledge, and understanding science, and such as had ability in them to stand in the king's palace, and whom they might teach the learning and the tongue of the Chaldeans. (Daniel 1:3–4)

Isolation

The king's first step in attempting to brainwash these guys was to try to *isolate* them from God's influence. If he could get them to stop praying, stop worshiping, stop talking about God, stop studying the Scriptures, or even to stop thinking about their living God, he would be closer to controlling their minds.

Daniel, Hananiah, Mishael, and Azariah understood what it meant to be under siege by a barbaric enemy. They experienced starvation, thirst, fears, and the destruction of their families and home. These boys were forced to grow up very quickly. Author Charles Swindoll in his book *Daniel: God's Pattern for the Future* colorfully describes this dramatic time in Daniel's life.

Imagine being a fourteen or fifteen year old boy, living hundreds of miles from your family, forced to take college level courses in a foreign language, constantly barraged by pagan philosophy, and surrounded by the intimidating sights and sounds of the big city. There's no going home. No summer vacation. Only day in, day out, brainwashing in the ways of the world. Daniel and his friends passed the test with flying colors.[3]

By removing Daniel and his friends from their normal life influences, Nebuchadnezzar could only hope that he and his world would become the major influence in their lives. The luxury he offered them by living in the palace could replace their dependence on their families. The introduction to a whole new set of accommodating gods could maybe help them to forget the living God of Israel. Somehow, someway, the king and his court had to get these young Hebrews to stop thinking like Israelites and start considering the benefits of becoming a Babylonian.

What you think about is what you love. If Satan can get us to just think about his world, he can get us to love his world. Obviously John understood this when he pled, "Love not the world, neither the things that are in the world. If any man love the world, the love of the Father is not in him. For all that is in the world, the lust of the flesh, and the lust of the eyes, and the pride of life, is not of the Father, but is of the world. And the world passeth away, and the lust thereof: but he that doeth the will of God abideth forever." (1 John 2:15–17)

Do you purposefully allow yourself to be *isolated* from godly influences? If you allow yourself to be isolated from the things of God, it is just a matter of time before you will choose such isolation as a way of life. When church attendance, Christian fellowship, and serious Bible study disappears from your life, you are closer to extinction than you realize.

The more you think about your Savior, the more you will love Him. Conversely, the less you think about your Savior, the less you will love Him. Isolation is scary. The consequences of such isolation are frightening. God provides numerous ways for us to live under His constant influence, but, sad to say, too many potential teen leaders choose isolation over influence. There really is no excuse for isolation, even in our hostile world. Here are three direct avenues of influence that God makes available to each of us.

The Influence of His Incredible Creation

When you consider the work of God's hands, you are reminded of His creative omnipotence. When you consider the heavens with its twinkling stars, unknowable planets, and glorious galaxies; the earth with its breathtaking sunsets, magnificent mountains, and secret worlds found deep within its oceans; the animal world hosting delicate humming birds, sleek cheetahs, and little maggot-like larva that God transforms into the beautiful monarch, you have to acknowledge His power and authority over our lives.

The Influence of His Indwelling Spirit

Through the comforting, convicting, and controlling work of God's Holy Spirit, you are influenced to walk in the Spirit and not after the lusts of the flesh. When God's Spirit is in control, the gratitude of our hearts will be expressed with a new song no one can silence.

The Influence of His Inspired Word

Through reading, personal study, memorization, meditation, preaching, singing, counseling, and sharing with friends, God uses His Word to influence the way you think by renewing our minds.

So you have to ask yourself some pretty tough questions.

- Do you purposefully isolate yourself from godly influences?

- In what ways do you isolate yourself from God's Word?

- Are you experiencing a lack of commitment (isolating yourself) to a Bible-preaching local church?

- In what ways do you resist (isolate yourself from) the influence of God's Spirit?

- In what ways do you ignore (isolate yourself from) the impact from God's creation?

The more you isolate yourself from God's influence, the quicker you will think and live like Babylonians. Now let's take a look at Nebuchadnezzar's second attempt to brainwash these four lion-like leaders through indoctrination.

Indoctrination

> And the king spake unto Ashpenaz the master of his eunuchs, that he should bring certain of the children of Israel, and of the king's seed, and of the princes; children in whom was no blemish, but well favoured, and skilful in all wisdom, and cunning in knowledge, and understanding science, and such as had ability in them to stand in the king's palace, and whom they might **teach the learning and the tongue of the Chaldeans**. And the king appointed them a daily provision of the king's meat, and of the wine which he drank: so nourishing them three years, that at the end thereof they might stand before the king. (Daniel 1:3–5)

There is nothing wrong in learning a new language and studying another culture unless you accept a culture that violates the Word of God or attacks the character of God. The world thrives on materialism, greed, popularity, acceptance, tolerance, and self-love. God's Word teaches a way of life that opposes such true worldliness.

Indoctrination is an attempt to teach someone to fully accept the ideas, opinions, and life philosophies of the indoctrinator without considering any other teaching. Indoctrination loves *uncritical* thinkers, or even better, *non-thinkers* who readily accept whatever and whenever, as long as these pseudo-thinkers do not stray far from their comfort zone.

Daniel did not take long to take his stand. "Eat from the king's menu? Eat what the king himself is eating? Would that be a big deal? We are in Babylon, far from our Jewish culture and kosher food. Come on, we have to eat in order to live, so I am sure this is one area that God would overlook." Not Daniel or his friends. He did not wait until the banquet was spread to decide. He made up his mind long before the delicious smells tantalized his teenage appetite.

What about the king's delicacies? Sinclair Ferguson again shares some unique insight to Daniel's dilemma.

> Perhaps what Daniel perceived (correctly) in this food allotment was an effort to seduce him into the lifestyle of a Babylonian through the enjoyment of pleasures he had never before known before. . . . The good life that Daniel was offered was intended by the king to wean him away from the hard life to which God had called him. It would encourage him to focus on himself and on a life of enjoyment. It would lead him to think of himself no longer as a servile Israelite but as a distinguished courtier.[4]

First Observation

How many teachers do you currently have? Who is your favorite teacher? Who is your least favorite teacher? (Don't say it out loud.) Whatever your educational experience—homeschool, private school, Christian school, public school—you can probably list about three to ten teachers in your life. You often forget about the many hours of real life classroom experience and what those teachers are trying to teach you online, on-screen, on the ball court, or even on the job. Admit it or not, you are in class most of your life. For instance, your comfort level with sin is under attack. In a world of tolerance, you are being taught that sin is not sinful anymore. Your professors for this course may be commentators on network news channels, comedians on late night TV, or the friends that you hang out with. All are teachers, many of whom want to indoctrinate you to think and live just like them.

Second Observation

Daniel often took a hard stand without being harsh; he always told the truth, but it was packaged in concern and compassion.

1. Daniel was sensitive to his supervisor Ashpenaz's dilemma and offered a Ten-Day-My-Flesh-Is-Fatter-Than-Your-Flesh Diet Plan. Daniel was a sensitive guy.

2. You can be sensitive to others without compromising your convictions. Saying "No thank you" to someone who offers you a beer or a cigarette is not compromise. The offer may be an act of kindness on their part. Your kind response may be a key into their hearts.

3. "Throughout Scripture you will find courageous people who had to defy authority in order to obey God, and in every case, they took the wise and gentle approach."[5] "If possible, so far as it depends on you, live peaceably with all" (Romans 12:18 ESV).

4. Daniel was committed to the truth, even if it was hard to do so, and he was honored because of it—by Nebuchadnezzar, by his daughter many years later, and by King Darius.

Third Observation

The greatest defense against the world's attempt to indoctrinate us is a solid, secure saturation with the Word of God.

1. "True faithfulness in Scripture is first exercised in small things and in private. If we fail there, any faithfulness we show in public will be hypocrisy, a performance for the crowd and not an expression of loyalty to our Lord."[6]

2. The families of these teen boys enjoyed living under the rule of godly King Josiah. Josiah was king of Judah for thirty-one years before King Nebuchadnezzar kidnapped Daniel and his friends.

3. Daniel was not without the Word of God. He knew of David's sin, of Joseph's resolve, and of Joshua's fears. He could often meditate on God's sovereign control and rest in the fact that God is an all-powerful, all-knowing, and all-gracious God.

Identification

Now among these were of the children of Judah, Daniel, Hananiah, Mishael, and Azariah: unto whom the prince of the eunuchs gave names: for he gave unto Daniel the name of Belteshazzar; and to Hananiah, of Shadrach; and to Mishael, of Meshach; and to Azariah, of Abednego. (Daniel 1:6–7)

Isolation didn't work. Daniel's lion-like character refused to be dulled by the king's indoctrination or intimidation techniques. Would a subtle change in identity do the job? Our personal identity is very important to us. There are few things in life as personal as our name given at birth. Nebuchadnezzar insisted that the four Hebrew POWs have their names changed. Instead of using the Hebrew words for Jehovah God (El-Jah-iah), their new names incorporated the names of Babylonian deities (Bel-Nabu).

- Daniel means "God is my judge," but his name was changed to Belteshazzar which means "Bel protect his life."

- Hananiah means "the Lord shows grace," but his new name Shadrach means "command of Aku" (the moongod).

- Mishael means "Who is like God?" His new name Meshach means "Who is as Aku is?"

- Azariah means "The Lord is my help," and Abednego means "Servant of Nebo (Nego)."

Although nicknames can be fun—Buck! Scar! Rocky! (mine was Humble Pie!)—a nickname could send the wrong message. "Hey guys, come on, you're one of us now." Who does not want to be totally accepted among their peers? A new name could give them the opportunity to conceal the fact that they were Israelites—followers of Jehovah God—if they allowed such to happen.

As they heard their names called day after day, it was an additional temptation for them to yield to the pressure to think of themselves as citizens of Babylon rather than of Jerusalem, . . . The fact that in the royal court could still remember that Daniel was Belteshazzar's real name is a testimony to the way that he continued to sing the Lord's song in a foreign land.[7]

Oh, for the courageous heart of Daniel, who held tightly onto the simple things that identified him to the cause of Jehovah God. A Marine proudly wears his dress blues. A soldier is honored to march in his uniform. But to hide the fact that you are a Christian seems to be quite acceptable today. Do you try to look like an unbeliever, talk like an unbeliever, or live like an unbeliever? What do you do or say that identifies you to your friends as a loyal follower of Jesus Christ?

Identification please! Even though state troopers request it, salesclerks check it, and airport security officers demand it, some still attempt to hide it. While some take great measures to protect themselves from identity theft, others give it away! As young Christian leaders, there are questions that need to be both asked and answered by those struggling or even embarrassed to be identified with our Lord Jesus Christ.

- How does baptism impact your identification with Christ?

- How does church membership and attendance affect your identification with Christ?

- How do your peers see that you are identified with Jesus Christ?

- Does your appearance in any way identify you with Babylon?

- Does most of your entertainment come from Jerusalem or Babylon?

- How does your language identify you with either Jerusalem or with Babylon?

- Are you ever embarrassed when one of your co-workers, school mates, or neighbors identifies you with Jesus Christ in a mocking way?

- Are you honored (and humbled) to be a Christian? Is it a joy to you to be identified with the Lord Jesus Christ?

- Do you believe the comforting truths of 2 Timothy 1:7–8?
  "For God hath not given us the spirit of fear; but of power, and of love, and of a sound mind. Be not thou therefore ashamed of the testimony of our Lord."

Those who purpose in their hearts to please God not only do so, but are respected by those who seek to sway them from their stand—"acceptable to God, and approved of men" (Romans 14:18). Do you have any regrets in the way you have walked with God over the last year? If you could go back in time and relive the past year, what would you change?

Once believers blend in with unbelievers, they lose their identity. Once they lose their identity, they lose their influence. Not so with Daniel, Hananiah, Mishael, and Azariah. Not only did these teens keep their hearts anchored in Jerusalem as they lived in Babylon, they kept their influence that is still impacting teens worldwide today.

Intimidation

What does it take to intimidate you? Are you easily controlled by those who threaten you? Reject you? Attack what you stand for? Daniel, Hananiah, Mishael, and Azariah faced manipulative intimidation on a daily basis. "Obey or be killed! Do what we say or die!" Intimidation is the result of letting fear, timidity, peer pressure, rejection, or unrealistic threats control what you do and who you are. Intimidation to compromise your convictions comes in many forms: mocking, ignoring, rejection, bullying, flattery, bribery, embarrassment, and even a welcoming acceptance into a new set of friends. You young lion-like leaders are challenged to respond in a way that is not natural. The pressure for you to compromise your convictions as you enter high school or college is at times almost unbearable. How can you refuse to be intimidated by intimidation? God! God is never intimidated. When you are emboldened by His presence your confidence can intimidate your intimidators.

Because Daniel, Mishael, Azariah, and Hananiah were young men with lion-like character, they refused to be intimidated by either the king or the chief eunuch's plea. Nothing seemed to lessen their resolve even though they could have been executed for refusing the king's commands. The kings of Daniel's day were outrageously out of control. Talk about "my way or the highway." If they did not have their own way, the consequences for everyone around were devastating.

> But Daniel purposed in his heart that he would not defile himself with the portion of the king's meat, nor with the wine which he drank: therefore he requested of the prince of the eunuchs that he might not defile himself. (Daniel 1:8)

> And the chief of the eunuchs said to Daniel, I fear my lord the king, who has appointed your food and drink. For why should he see your faces looking worse than the young men who are your age? Then you would endanger my head before the king. (Daniel 1:10 NKJV)

> The king answered and said to the Chaldeans, The thing is gone from me: if ye will not make known unto me the dream, with the interpretation thereof, ye shall be cut in pieces, and your houses shall be made a dunghill. (Daniel 2:5)

> For this cause the king was angry and very furious, and commanded to destroy all the wise men of Babylon. And the decree went forth that the wise men should be slain; and they sought Daniel and his fellows to be slain. (Daniel 2:12–13)

Then a herald cried aloud: "To you it is commanded, O peoples, nations, and languages, that at the time you hear the sound of the horn, flute, harp, lyre, and psaltery, in symphony with all kinds of music, you shall fall down and worship the gold image that King Nebuchadnezzar has set up; and whoever does not fall down and worship shall be cast immediately into the midst of a burning fiery furnace. (Daniel 3:4–6 NKJV)

Then Nebuchadnezzar was full of fury, and the expression on his face changed toward Shadrach, Meshach, and Abednego. He spoke and commanded that they heat the furnace seven times more than it was usually heated. (Daniel 3:19 NKJV)

So these governors and satraps thronged before the king, and said thus to him: "King Darius, live forever! All the governors of the kingdom, the administrators and satraps, the counselors and advisors, have consulted together to establish a royal statute and to make a firm decree, that whoever petitions any god or man for thirty days, except you, O king, shall be cast into the den of lions." (Daniel 6:6–7 NKJV)

Throughout history, cruel intimidation from the world has been conquered by faith. Today, some think that peer pressure is too much to endure. Most would change their minds if they took a few minutes to compare the pressure they face with Hebrews 11-type of pressure.

Who through faith . . . stopped the mouths of lions, quenched the violence of fire, escaped the edge of the sword, out of weakness were made strong, waxed valiant in fight, turned to flight the armies of the aliens. Women received their dead raised to life again: and others were tortured, not accepting deliverance; . . . others had trial of cruel mockings and scourgings, . . . bonds and imprisonment: they were stoned, they were sawn asunder, were tempted, were slain with the sword: they wandered about in sheepskins and goatskins; being destitute, afflicted, tormented; (Of whom the world was not worthy;) they wandered in deserts . . . mountains, . . . and caves. (Hebrews 11:33–38)

I love that phrase, "of whom the world was not worthy." Those who find satisfaction in their own little worlds by mocking those who are different, torturing those who are seemingly inferior, and ridiculing those who believe differently are of little worth compared to those they mock, torture, and ridicule. Your worth in Christ as a child of God cannot be diminished by the foolish words of foolish people. Trust God and watch your faith fight fear.

Fear fears faith! Intimidation is intimidated and frightened by faith! If you would simply trust God and not fear men, bullies would become an endangered species. When you are intimate with God you will not be intimidated by man.

If you could only cry out with David, "The Lord is on my side. I will not fear: what can man do unto me?" (Psalm 118:6) and believe it! A secure awareness of God's presence and power is intimidation-proof.

Four Stabilizing Truths[8]

If you want to walk in the midst of enemy intimidators with an intimidation-proof vest on, memorize and meditate on these wonderful truths from God's Word.

1. God's love for me will never change.

> Who shall separate us from the love of Christ? shall tribulation, or distress, or persecution, or famine, or nakedness, or peril, or sword? As it is written, For thy sake we are killed all the day long; we are accounted as sheep for the slaughter. Nay, in all these things we are more than conquerors through Him that loved us. For I am persuaded, that neither death, nor life, nor angels, nor principalities, nor powers, nor things present, nor things to come, nor height, nor depth, nor any other creature, shall be able to separate us from the love of God, which is in Christ Jesus our Lord. (Romans 8:35–39)

The Lord hath appeared of old unto me, saying, Yea, I have loved thee with an everlasting love: therefore with loving-kindness have I drawn thee. (Jeremiah 31:3)

For God so loved the world, that he gave his only begotten Son, that whosoever believeth in him should not perish, but have everlasting life. For God sent not his Son into the world to condemn the world; but that the world through him might be saved. (John 3:16–17)

But God commendeth His love toward us, in that, while we were yet sinners, Christ died for us. (Romans 5:8)

In this was manifested the love of God toward us, because that God sent his only begotten Son into the world, that we might live through him. Herein is love, not that we loved God, but that he loved us, and sent his Son to be the propitiation for our sins. (1 John 4:9–10)

We love Him, because He first loved us. (1 John 4:19)

2. God's purpose for me is Christlikeness.

And we know that all things work together for good to them that love God, to them who are the called according to his purpose. For whom he did foreknow, he also did predestinate to be conformed to the image of his Son, that he might be the firstborn among many brethren. (Romans 8:28–29)

But put ye on the Lord Jesus Christ, and make not provision for the flesh, to fulfil the lusts thereof. (Romans 13:14)

But we all, with open face beholding as in a glass the glory of the Lord, are changed into the same image from glory to glory, even as by the Spirit of the Lord. (2 Corinthians 3:18)

Let this mind be in you, which was also in Christ Jesus: who, being in the form of God, thought it not robbery to be equal with God: but made himself of no reputation, and took upon him the form of a servant, and was made in the likeness of men: and being found in fashion as a man, he humbled himself, and became obedient unto death, even the death of the cross. Wherefore God also hath highly exalted him, and given him a name which is above every name: that at the name of Jesus every knee should bow, of things in heaven, and things in earth, and things under the earth; and that every tongue should confess that Jesus Christ is Lord, to the glory of God the Father. (Philippians 2:5–11)

Come unto me, all ye that labor and are heavy laden, and I will give you rest. Take my yoke upon you, and learn of me; for I am meek and lowly in heart: and ye shall find rest unto your souls. For my yoke is easy, and my burden is light. (Matthew 11:28–30)

For I have given you an example, that ye should do as I have done to you. (John 13:15)

He that saith he abideth in Him ought himself also so to walk, even as he walked. (1 John 2:6)

Be ye followers of me, even as I also am of Christ. (1 Corinthians 11:1)

3. God's Word for me is the final right answer.

All scripture is given by inspiration of God, and is profitable for doctrine, for reproof, for correction, for instruction in righteousness: that the man of God may be perfect, throughly furnished unto all good works. (2 Timothy 3:16–17)

But be ye doers of the word, and not hearers only, deceiving your own selves. For if any be a hearer of the word, and not a doer, he is like unto a man beholding his natural face in a glass: for he beholdeth himself, and goeth his way, and straightway forgetteth what manner of man he was. But whoso looketh into the perfect law of liberty, and continueth therein, he being not a forgetful hearer, but a doer of the work, this man shall be blessed in his deed. (James 1:22–25)

Therefore whosoever heareth these sayings of mine, and doeth them, I will liken him unto a wise man, which built his house upon a rock: and the rain descended, and the floods came, and the winds blew, and beat upon that house; and it fell not: for it was founded upon a rock. And every one that heareth these sayings of mine, and doeth them not, shall be likened unto a foolish man, which built his house upon the sand: and the rain descended, and the floods came, and the winds blew, and beat upon that house; and it fell: and great was the fall of it. (Matthew 7:24–27)

For whatsoever things were written aforetime were written for our learning, that we through patience and comfort of the scriptures might have hope. (Romans 15:4)

For the word of God is quick, and powerful, and sharper than any two-edged sword, piercing even to the dividing asunder of soul and spirit, and of the joints and marrow, and is a discerner of the thoughts and intents of the heart. (Hebrews 4:12)

Thy word is a lamp unto my feet, and a light unto my path. (Psalm 119:105)

The statutes of the Lord are right, rejoicing the heart: the commandment of the Lord is pure, enlightening the eyes. (Psalm 19:8)

4. God's grace for me is always sufficient.

For the grace of God that bringeth salvation hath appeared to all men, teaching us that, denying ungodliness and worldly lusts, we should live soberly, righteously, and godly, in this present world; looking for that blessed hope, and the glorious appearing of the great God and our Savior Jesus Christ; Who gave himself for us, that he might redeem us from all iniquity, and purify unto himself a peculiar people, zealous of good works. (Titus 2:11–14)

Being justified freely by his grace through the redemption that is in Christ Jesus. (Romans 3:24)

Moreover the law entered, that the offence might abound. But where sin abounded, grace did much more abound: that as sin hath reigned unto death, even so might grace reign through righteousness unto eternal life by Jesus Christ our Lord. (Romans 5:20-21)

But by the grace of God I am what I am: and his grace which was bestowed upon me was not in vain; but I labored more abundantly than they all: yet not I, but the grace of God which was with me. (1 Corinthians 15:10)

And He said unto me, My grace is sufficient for thee: for my strength is made perfect in weakness. Most gladly therefore will I rather glory in my infirmities, that the power of Christ may rest upon me. Therefore I take pleasure in infirmities, in reproaches, in necessities, in persecutions, in distresses for Christ's sake: for when I am weak, then am I strong. (2 Corinthians 12:9–10)

In whom we have redemption through his blood, the forgiveness of sins, according to the riches of his grace. (Ephesians 1:7)

For by grace are ye saved through faith; and that not of yourselves: it is the gift of God: not of works, lest any man should boast. (Ephesians 2:8–9)

Grace be with all them that love our Lord Jesus Christ in sincerity. Amen. (Ephesians 6:24)

Thou therefore, my son, be strong in the grace that is in Christ Jesus. (2 Timothy 2:1)

But he giveth more grace. Wherefore he saith, God resisteth the proud, but giveth grace unto the humble. Submit yourselves therefore to God. Resist the devil, and he will flee from you. Draw nigh to God, and He will draw nigh to you. Cleanse your hands, ye sinners; and purify your hearts, ye double minded. (James 4:6–8)

And God is able to make all grace abound toward you; that ye, always having all sufficiency in all things, may abound to every good work. (2 Corinthians 9:8)

Again, fear fears faith! Intimidation is intimidated and frightened by faith! When you are intimate with God, you will not be intimidated by man.

Kidnapped? Yes. Brainwashed? No! Daniel, Hananiah, Mishael, and Azariah were young men with lion-like character who refused to be brainwashed. They did not allow *isolation* to break them; they refused to be *indoctrinated* by worldly, unbiblical thinking; they were not intimidated by *intimidation* and by faith stayed strong; finally, they were pleased to be *identified* with Israel and Jehovah God and did not allow their identities to be changed or altered just to fit in with their new surroundings. Easy? No. Satisfying? Definitely. Regrets? No!

In some ways, it almost feels like you are already prisoners of war in a hostile country. The Babylonian world was not too much different from what you are facing in your God-defiant world today. For those who do not defy God, they ignore God and if they had their way, those of you who desire to live your life pleasing to the one, eternal, almighty God would be eliminated as quickly as possible.

Godly lives make ungodly people uncomfortable. So for the world to remain inside their own man-made comfort level, they must either get rid of you or get you to join their world—*annihilate* or *assimilate*.

If you were actually captured and thrown into a disgusting prison cell to rot and eventually die, here is a simple guide to keep the real you—your heart—from caving in to your enemy's wishes. They may someday destroy your body, but they cannot touch your heart and mind as you focus on your wonderful Lord and claim His precious promises.

And by the way, some prisons are made of stone and some include steel bars. Spiritual prisons can imprison any of us through rejection, lust, anger, bitterness, depression, or fear.

If you feel enslaved by any such *prisons*, this "Spiritual POW Survival Guide" will help you to keep a heart like Daniel and his friends.

Spiritual POW Survival Guide[9]

Establish a Spiritual Hiding Place

When life's pressures and temptations seem unbearable, force your focus off the temptations or pressures and purposefully focus on your *faithful, loving, heavenly Father*. When your peers are unrelenting and the loneliness of rejection begins to overwhelm your heart, force your mind off the peers, off the rejection, off the loneliness, and think about your *faithful, loving, heavenly Father*. Literally, say those four words so you can hear them both in your mind and in your heart—faithful, loving, heavenly, Father; faithful, loving, heavenly, Father; faithful, loving, heavenly, Father; faithful, loving, heavenly, Father.

Now repeat these powerful word-truths a few more times, but this time pause at every comma, thinking about what you just said. Faithful (pause and think), loving (pause and think), heavenly (pause and think some more), Father (pause and think still some more). Don't be afraid to repeat this simple meditation exercise over and over until your mind is comforted by your faithful, loving, heavenly Father.

As you establish a spiritual hiding place in your heart, you will find yourself running to it each time life's pressures cause a feeling of *emotional claustrophobia* in your life. Most run to pity, depression, anger, doubt, or hopelessness rather than remembering that you are not alone, you are not unloved; you have a faithful, loving, heavenly Father.

Daniel did this.

Now when Daniel knew that the writing was signed, he went into his house; and his windows being open in his chamber toward Jerusalem, he kneeled upon his knees three times a day, and prayed, and gave thanks before his God, as he did aforetime. (Daniel 6:10)

David did this.

Thou art my hiding place; Thou shalt preserve me from trouble; thou shalt compass me about with songs of deliverance. Selah. (Psalm 32:7)

You can too.

Thou art my hiding place and my shield: I hope in thy word. (Psalm 119:114)

Cope with Rejection

Others have survived rejection and you can too. Maybe rejection is God's way of protecting you from greater hurt down the road. Pray for pity and learn to feel sorry for the insecure, selfish people that are rejecting you—if you watch their world long enough you will see that it is just a matter of time before they will be rejected too. Also, think of those who will never reject you—no matter what! Finally, remind yourself what happened to your Lord Jesus Christ. He came to His own, and they did not receive Him but rejected Him, mocked Him, beat Him, and crucified Him. Jesus knew how to cope with rejection and as you consider Him, you can too.

Hananiah, Mishael, and Azariah did this.

Shadrach, Meshach, and Abednego answered and said to the king, "O Nebuchadnezzar, we have no need to answer you in this matter. If that is the case, our God whom we serve is able to deliver us from the burning fiery furnace, and He will deliver us from your hand, O king. But if not, let it be known to you, O king, that we do not serve your gods, nor will we worship the gold image which you have set up." (Daniel 3:16–18)

Jesus did this.

He is despised and rejected of men; a man of sorrows, and acquainted with grief: and we hid as it were our faces from Him; He was despised, and we esteemed Him not. (Isaiah 53:3)

You can too.

Blessed are ye, when men shall revile you, and persecute you, and shall say all manner of evil against you falsely, for my sake. (Matthew 5:11)

Engage Your Mind

You are not what you think you are, but you are what you think. If you continue to tell yourself that life is not fair, people are not fair, and God is not fair, you will live a lonely, sad, and depressing life. Keeping your mind engaged by thinking, learning, and actively working is crucial in surviving this hostile world. There is plenty of pain, death, hurt, and fear to think about. Don't let such thinking control your mind. Learn the positive approach to thinking that Paul emphasizes in Philippians 4:8–9: "Finally, brethren, whatever things are true, whatever things are noble, whatever things are just, whatever things are pure, whatever things are lovely, whatever things are of good report, if there is any virtue and if there is anything praiseworthy—meditate [think] on these things. The things which you learned and received and heard and saw in me, these do, and the God of peace will be with you" (NKJV).

God's creativity is amazing. There is so much to learn and to do you could not get it all in if you lived fifty lifetimes. For example, read. Read to learn; read for fun; read to grow; read! Learn how to play the piano, a guitar, or a mandolin. Learn to speak Spanish, French, Italian, or Yugoslavian. Take violin, flute, clarinet, or accordion lessons. Take up woodworking, weight lifting, running, Ti-Quan-Leap. Take courses on becoming a nursing assistant. Work with a plumber or electrician and learn their trade. Memorize the book of Philippians. Take up disc golf, running, or painting. Get a job walking dogs (or cats)! Engage your mind. Make an effort to control the way that you think rather than allowing your thoughts to control the way you live.

Daniel and his friends did this:

> Then the king instructed Ashpenaz, the master of his eunuchs, to bring some of the children of Israel and some of the king's descendants and some of the nobles, young men in whom there was no blemish, but good-looking, gifted in all wisdom, possessing knowledge and quick to understand, who had ability to serve in the king's palace, and whom they might teach the language and literature of the Chaldeans.
> . . . And in all matters of wisdom and understanding about which the king examined them, he found them ten times better than all the magicians and astrologers who were in all his realm. (Daniel 1:3–4, 20 NKJV)

You are all commanded to this:

> And if any man think that he knoweth anything, he knoweth nothing yet as he ought to know. (1 Corinthians 8:2)

You can too.

> Finally, brethren, whatsoever things are true, whatsoever things are honest, whatsoever things are just, whatsoever things are pure, whatsoever things are lovely, whatsoever things are of good report; if there be any virtue, and if there be any praise, think on these things. (Philippians 4:8)

Cast All Your Cares on God

Release your cares, anxieties, worries, and discouragements to God. If you try to play catch with your Lord Jesus Christ, you will soon learn that He never throws your troubles back to you! When God asked Peter to write, "Casting all your care upon him; for he careth for you" (1 Peter 5:7), He meant it! Cast; throw; let go! Cast every fear to God, knowing that He is almighty. Cast every anxious thought God's way, remembering that God is sovereign and in control. Each time you are tempted to get down and depressed, cast those thoughts to God knowing that He loves you and wants the best for you! Remember, He is your faithful, loving, heavenly Father.

Daniel and his friends did this.

Then Daniel went to his house, and made the decision known to Hananiah, Mishael, and Azariah, his companions, that they might seek mercies from the God of heaven concerning this secret, so that Daniel and his companions might not perish with the rest of the wise men of Babylon. Then the secret was revealed to Daniel in a night vision. So Daniel blessed the God of heaven. (Daniel 2:17–19 NKJV)

Peter did this.

Casting all your care upon him; for he careth for you. (1 Peter 5:7)

You can too.

Be careful for nothing; but in everything by prayer and supplication with thanksgiving let your requests be made known unto God. (Philippians 4:6)

RESIST LIVING A LIFE OF INSANITY

—————•—————

DANIEL 2 AND 4

Immunize Yourself from Mad Cow Disease

Daniel 4:33 gives us the picture of Nebuchadnezzar at possibly his worst moment in life. He "was driven from men, and did eat grass as oxen, and his body was wet with the dew of heaven, till his hairs were grown like eagles' feathers, and his nails like birds' claws."

What Is Mad Cow Disease?

In 1986 some cows in Great Britain began drooling and staggering while others became incredibly aggressive. Mad cow disease is technically a fatal brain disease called *bonine spongiform encephalopathy* (BSE). This infectious disease shoots the brain full of holes making it look like a sponge. Humans get a variant of this disease which starts with mood swings, numbness, and uncontrolled body movements and results with destruction of the brain, somewhat like Alzheimer's.

The cause was traced back to a feeding practice where dead cattle were ground up and added to the cattle's feed to increase protein in their diet.

The cows were feeding on themselves.

The Sad Tale of Kuru

Laughing death, locally called *kuru*, was a progressive, fatal brain malady that robbed its victims of the ability to walk, talk, and even eat. *Kuru* produced a Swiss-cheesing of the brain that killed dozens of tribal people in New Guinea, and the epidemic was not controlled until there was a reduction in the deadly feuds between the villages and cannibalism was stopped.

Why? Because village rites often honored close relatives (wanting them to remain with them) by eating their internal organs when they died. Within a tribe, such meals transmitted the kuru infection either while the bodies were handled or when the relative's remains were eaten.

The victims were feeding on themselves.

Insanity occurs when someone loses his normal reasoning ability. There are several Greek words used in the New Testament for *insanity*. The Greek word *mainomai* is the root word for the English word *mania*, and it describes a diseased mental condition. Another Greek word for *insanity* is *ekstasis* or *exhistemi*, which means the "behavior of a person who is no longer controlled by his normal reason."[1]

The Hebrew word used in the Old Testament for *insanity* is *shaga)*, which means, "be mad or madness." It has been connected with an Arabic word *saga'a* meaning "the ceaseless cooing of pigeons," and connected with an Assyrian word (*segu*) meaning "to howl or rage."[2]

Insanity is an expression of extreme folly or unreasonableness or absurd lunacy. It demonstrates madness, craziness, senselessness, and foolhardiness. It is technically an unsoundness of mind.

Just as mad cow disease comes from cow's feeding on themselves and kuru comes from cannibalism, *spiritual insanity* comes from a constant diet of self.

The Cause of Spiritual Insanity—Selfish Pride

All this came upon the king Nebuchadnezzar. At the end of twelve months he walked in the palace of the kingdom of Babylon. The king spake, and said, **Is not this great Babylon, that I have built for the house of the kingdom by the might of my power, and for the honor of my majesty?** While the word was in the king's mouth, there fell a voice from heaven, saying, O king Nebuchadnezzar, to thee it is spoken; the kingdom is departed from thee. And they shall drive thee from men, and thy dwelling shall be with the beasts of the field: they shall make thee to eat grass as oxen, and seven times shall pass over thee, until thou know that the most High ruleth in the kingdom of men, and giveth it to whomsoever He will. (Daniel 4:28–32)

For those who are consumed with self, it is just a matter of time before insanity sets in.

Everyone who insists on living a life that rejects or ignores God can be assured that God will give them over to what they want—a life without God . . . a life of insanity. It is insane to reject a sovereign, loving God. The more depraved a man becomes, the more insane he becomes. It is a lose-lose situation.

Romans 1 reveals the simple digression that takes place when we—God's creation—begin worshiping ourselves instead of God. Self-worship is the realistic result of selfishness.

For the wrath of God is revealed from heaven against all ungodliness and unrighteousness of men, who suppress the truth in unrighteousness, because what may be known of God is manifest in them, for God has shown it to them. For since the creation of the world His invisible attributes are clearly seen, being understood by the things that are made, even His eternal power and Godhead, so that they are without excuse, because, although they knew God, they did not glorify Him as God, nor were thankful, but became futile in their thoughts, and their foolish hearts were darkened. Professing to be wise, they became fools, and changed the glory of the incorruptible God into an image made like corruptible man—and birds and four-footed animals and creeping things. Therefore God also gave them up to uncleanness, in the lusts of their hearts, to dishonor their bodies among themselves, who exchanged the truth of God for the lie, and worshiped and served the creature rather than the Creator, who is blessed forever. Amen. For this reason God gave them up to vile passions. For even their women exchanged the natural use for what is against nature. Likewise also the men, leaving the natural use of the woman, burned in their lust for one another, men with men committing what is shameful, and receiving in themselves the penalty of their error which was due. And even as they did not like to retain God in their knowledge, God gave them over to a debased mind, to do those things which are not fitting; being filled with all unrighteousness, sexual immorality, wickedness, covetousness, maliciousness; full of envy, murder, strife, deceit, evil-mindedness; they are whisperers, backbiters, haters of God, violent, proud, boasters, inventors of evil things, disobedient to parents, undiscerning, untrustworthy, unloving, unforgiving, unmerciful; who, knowing the righteous judgment of God, that those who practice such things are deserving of death, not only do the same but also approve of those who practice them. (Romans 1:18–32 NKJV)

Desire—instant gratification; "Give me what I want when I want it!" God uses the sin of immorality to illustrate instant gratification. Those who are addicted to instant gratification quickly give in to their sexual desires and believe that there are no rules, no need to wait, and no one who can tell them "no." They instantaneously fulfill whatever desire they have.

Deviant Desires—diminished gratification; "The buzz is gone." Gratifying their desires no longer satisfies and leads to perversion—satisfaction in a man-made way (in a way God never intended)—involving the self-love of pornography, extra-marital affairs, premarital sex, homosexuality, child abuse, incest, and the list goes on and on.

Depraved Desires—reprobate gratification; Instead of being ashamed of their depravity and deviant behavior, those who reject God insist that all—including God—should think that what they are doing is right! This is insane!

How low can a man go?

> The same hour was the thing fulfilled upon Nebuchadnezzar: and he was driven from men, and did eat grass as oxen, and his body was wet with the dew of heaven, till his hairs were grown like eagles' feathers, and his nails like birds' claws. (Daniel 4:33)

Nebuchadnezzar lifted himself as high as he could—a god. God lowered him to the lowest he could and still keep him alive—an animal. What is the life of a wild dog? He doesn't care what he looks like, and he doesn't care about the other dogs in the pack. He lives for two things: (1) he eats to survive and will kill to do so, and (2) he looks for a female dog in heat. They live to satisfy their desires for food and sex and nothing else. I have personally known some dogs that seem to be much better trained than some men.

Peter and Jude, under the inspiration of our all-knowing God, speak of a spiritual insanity that is likened to wild, ravenous animals.

> But these, as natural brute beasts [as irrational animals, creatures of instinct], made to be taken and destroyed, speak evil [blaspheming] of the things that they understand not; and shall utterly perish in their own corruption; . . . having eyes full of adultery, and that cannot cease from sin; beguiling unstable souls: an heart they have exercised with covetous practices; cursed children. (2 Peter 2:12, 14)

Wild dogs, mad cows, kuru, and the prideful King Nebuchadnezzar each leave us an example of what can happen to those who live on a constant diet of self. They are destined for ruin. They are all on a path to insanity.

The king thought, "Is not this Babylon that I have built . . . by the might of my power . . . for the honour of my majesty?" (Daniel 4:30).

In three concise statements, King Nebuchadnezzar revealed his selfish heart. His pride said, "I have built"; his self-sufficiency bragged, "by my power"; and his self-glory boasted, "for the honor of my majesty."

You may never stagger and drool; you may never eat grass like a cow; you may never bark and howl as a dog. But if you live on a constant diet of self and walk in pride, you will go spiritually insane.

Our selfishness is something that we are either blinded to or refuse to deal with. Someone has said that you never know you are selfish until you get married; then you really don't know how selfish you are until you have kids. Basically, whenever you are responsible for anyone other than yourself, your selfishness is magnified, and you have a real-life battle to face.

Pride is always at war with humility. Humility recognizes that God and others are the ones actually responsible for all the good you have done or achievements you have accomplished. Once our focus begins to lean away from God or others, we are back on the path to extreme selfishness and utter insanity.

Here is a simple way to remove the blinders to personal selfishness. Even if we think we are doing OK in the humility battle, it is good to be a bit introspective. So ask yourself or ask someone you trust to answer questions like these.

- "Is there anything in my life that would cause concern for my future purity?"
- "Do others trust me? Should I trust myself?"

- "Would anyone question my sincerity? Do I ever come across as a phony or with a hypocritical attitude?"
- "How's my prayer life?"

The Cure for Spiritual Insanity— True Humility

To immunize yourself from mad cow disease, kuru, or Nebuchadnezzar-like insanity, you need to give yourself two spiritual shots in the arm.

Immunization Shot #1
Refocus—take your eyes completely off self.

Immunization Shot #2
Refocus—turn your eyes to your amazing God by meditating on His marvelous attributes along with the overwhelming needs of others.

> And at the end of the days I Nebuchadnezzar lifted up mine eyes unto heaven, and mine understanding returned unto me, and I blessed the most High, and I praised and honored him that liveth forever, whose dominion is an everlasting dominion, and his kingdom is from generation to generation: and all the inhabitants of the earth are reputed as nothing: and he doeth according to his will in the army of heaven, and among the inhabitants of the earth: and none can stay his hand, or say unto him, What doest thou? At the same time my reason returned unto me; and for the glory of my kingdom, mine honour and brightness returned unto me; and my counselors and my lords sought unto me; and I was established in my kingdom, and excellent majesty was added unto me. Now I Nebuchadnezzar praise and extol and honor the King of heaven, all whose works are truth, and his ways judgment: and those that walk in pride he is able to abase. (Daniel 4:34–37)

- He understood who God is.

- He humbled himself before God.

- He sensed God's blessings.

- He gave God His proper worth.

- He honored God.

- He understood God's sovereignty.

- He realized God is in control.

- He knew God's ways are true and just.

- He saw man's frailty in light of God.

We all struggle with selfish and stubborn pride on some level. When King Nebuchadnezzar reversed his egotistical focus to a God focus, he began to see both himself and God more clearly. He finally realized who God was, and who he was not. You must do the same if you are to keep yourself from a spiritual mad cow disease. Does your heart mirror the heart of a humbled Nebuchadnezzar?

- Do you really understand who God is?

- Have you volitionally humbled yourself before God?

- Do you sense God's blessings on a daily basis?

- Have you given God His proper worth and expressed it to others?

- Do you honor God with your life?

- Do you really understand God's sovereignty?

- Do you understand and realize that God is in control?

- Do you know that God's ways are true and just?

- Do you see your frailty in light of God's magnificence?

There are a number of great books on humility; there are Bible studies dedicated to the study of pride and humility; there are multiple verses in Scripture to memorize on humility, but if you are going to truly understand humility in the context of your self-centered world and self-gratifying flesh, you must study and meditate on what our Lord Jesus Christ did for us when He "humbled himself, and became obedient unto death, even the death of the cross." If you take the time to memorize and meditate on Philippians 2:8, you will understand humility in a new way.

Spiritual insanity comes from a constant diet of self.

Spiritual maturity comes from a high view of God.

DANIEL PRINCIPLE THREE

ENDURE INTENSE
PEER PRESSURE
———————•———————

DANIEL 3:1–30

Be Prepared to Take the Heat

2 Timothy 3:12 states that "All that will live godly in Christ Jesus shall suffer persecution." In your desire to personally keep lion-like leaders from making it to the endangered species list, as you mature and increase in godliness, you will experience an increase in persecution. Because godly living is politically incorrect in a world that is hostile toward God, persecution may come in the form of threats, intimidations, political bullying, and even physical harm. Because godly living is unpopular in a world that hates God's people, persecution may come in the form of rejection, lies, and false accusations. Godly living in Christ Jesus equals persecution!

Daniel 3 is all about love, loyalty, leadership, and loneliness. King Nebuchadnezzar and the Chaldean leaders were motivated by love and loyalty—for themselves. Azariah, Mishael, and Hananiah were motivated by love and loyalty —toward God. The result is seen in the impact of their leadership on others. Those loyal to God changed the focus of an entire nation from Nebuchadnezzar's golden image to an intensely hot furnace in just seconds. Instead of seeing how great the king of Babylon was, all saw the power and greatness of the living King of Heaven. Godly, lion-like leaders will ultimately help all under their influence to see God more clearly.

If Daniel 3 was viewed as a play, and you were assigned to give the character analysis of the three major actors, you would first have to take a close look at King Nebuchadnezzar, then the Chaldeans, and finally the three Hebrew slaves in exile. It is obvious that the king and the Chaldeans thought they had the Hebrews outnumbered and outranked. They forgot about the God of the Hebrews.

Living Godly in Christ Jesus Will Never Be Politically Correct!

Nebuchadnezzar the king made an image of gold.
(Daniel 3:1)

> How quickly the king took his dream's focus on the eternal power of an almighty King and attempted to put the focus back on his own kingdom and kingship. The Septuagint says that Nebuchadnezzar built the statue in the eighteenth year of his reign—sixteen years after Daniel's interpretation of the king's dream in chapter 2. In all that time, none of those prophecies have come true. There's been no "silver" kingdom and no "bronze" kingdom. There was no "iron" kingdom and certainly no sign of a magical flying stone. So pumped up with a renewed sense of invincibility, the king thumbs his nose at God and builds a massive idol as a glittering symbol of his sovereign rule. The figure is every bit the colossus that he saw in his dream, except the entire image is overlaid in gold (not just the head)—and you can be sure the feet have not a trace of clay. No kingdom, natural or supernatural, is going to crush his statue . . . or his empire.[1]

King Nebuchadnezzar is still insane! Here is a man that thinks he can thwart God's plan and change the future after a slight peek into what was nothing more to him than Daniel's crystal ball. He refused to take God seriously—at least for a while.

Instead of just the head of gold, he now overlays the entire image in gold signifying that his kingdom will be greater than the silver, bronze, and the iron kingdoms that were to follow.

Interestingly, Nebuchadnezzar's recreation of his dream of the ninety-foot golden statue left out some very important parts—the parts he did not want to believe would ever come true. He was not willing to admit that his glory would fade, certainly not to inferior armies and nations. Why didn't Nebuchnezzar tell the whole story?

- Where were the chest and arms of silver?

- Where were the belly and thighs of bronze?

- Where were the legs of iron?

- Where were the feet of iron and clay?

- Where was the stone that broke everything else in pieces?

Then a herald cried aloud: "To you it is commanded, O peoples, nations, and languages, that at the time you hear the sound of the horn, flute, harp, lyre, and psaltery, in symphony with all kinds of music, you shall fall down and worship the gold image that King Nebuchadnezzar has set up; and whoever does not fall down and worship shall be cast immediately into the midst of a burning fiery furnace." (Daniel 3:4–6 NKJV)

Nebuchadnezzar was not satisfied to be a king. He wanted to be a god! As the king of his own kingdom, as the sovereign of his own life, he was not willing to admit or acknowledge that there was a sovereign God. Even today, too many teens fight the concept of God's sovereignty. They want for themselves that which only God possesses. They want total say and control of their own lives. They want to be their own sovereign gods.

Nebuchadnezzar was not content to be obeyed; he wanted to be worshiped! The atmosphere for a choreographed worship service is set in motion. Only the best musicians are gathered to set the mood with a musical performance that can be experienced very few other places in the kingdom. The sheer magnificence of the golden image with all the beauty of the royal surroundings must have been a sight to behold.

The devil's way of worship is much like the modern day feel-good worship so prevalent today. He is still saying, "All these things I will give You, if You fall down and worship me" (Matthew 4:9 NASB).

Hananiah, Mishael, and Azariah did not want the acceptance of the selfish king or his puppet Chaldeans. They refused to bow, and the tattletale Chaldeans ran to the king with their accusing fingers all pointed at Daniel's three godly friends. "O King! O King! O King!"

> Wherefore at that time certain Chaldeans came near, and accused the Jews. They spake and said to the king Nebuchadnezzar, O king, live for ever. Thou, O king, hast made a decree, that every man that shall hear the sound of the cornet, flute, harp, sackbut, psaltery, and dulcimer, and all kinds of musick, shall fall down and worship the golden image: and whoso falleth not down and worshippeth, that he should be cast into the midst of a burning fiery furnace. There are certain Jews whom thou hast set over the affairs of the province of Babylon, Shadrach, Meshach, and Abednego; these men, O king, have not regarded thee: they serve not thy gods, nor worship the golden image which thou hast set up. Then Nebuchadnezzar in his rage and fury commanded to bring Shadrach, Meshach, and Abednego. Then they brought these men before the king. Nebuchadnezzar spake and said unto them, Is it true, O Shadrach, Meshach, and Abednego, do not ye serve my gods, nor worship the golden image which I have set up? Now if ye be ready that at what time ye hear the sound of the cornet, flute, harp, sackbut, psaltery, and dulcimer, and all kinds of musick, ye fall down and worship the image which I have made; well: but if ye worship not, ye shall be cast the same hour into the midst

of a burning fiery furnace; and who is that God that shall deliver you out of my hands? (Daniel 3:8–15)

"Who is that God that shall deliver you?" Both the king and his malicious Chaldeans are about to find out. Wouldn't you love to live with the confidence of Shadrach, Meshach, and Abednego? I promise you, their confidence was never self-confidence, but God-confidence. They were confident that God would deliver them—either *from* the fire or *through* the fire. Look at their response to this furious king.

Shadrach, Meshach, and Abednego, answered and said to the king, O Nebuchadnezzar, we are not careful [we have no need] to answer thee in this matter. If it be so, our God whom we serve is able to deliver us from the burning fiery furnace, and he will deliver us out of thine hand, O king. But if not, be it known to thee, O king that we will not serve thy gods, nor worship the golden image which thou hast set up. (Daniel 3:16–18)

Instead of the king being *deified* he is *defied*! And his childish response clearly shows his deceived heart.

Nebuchadnezzar was angry. Mad! As a king, he took pride that he controlled much of the known world, but he could not control his own rage. This is sad.

Nebuchadnezzar was:

- out of control—"rage and fury . . . full of fury" (Daniel 3:13,19)

- visibly upset—"the expression on his faced changed/ form of his visage" (Daniel 3:19 NKJV/KJV)

- unreasonable—"heat the furnace seven times more than it was usually heated" (Daniel 3:19 NKJV) (which actually would ease the torture by immediate death rather than being tortured in a slow cooker)

- impulsive—"the king's commandment was urgent" (Daniel 3:22) (acting without thinking)

Hananiah, Mishael, and Azariah were enslaved under such a king. What he said not only impacted their lives but their deaths also. The circumstances and context of the situation could not have been more difficult. If living under such a king was not bad enough, think about the pressure put on by the selfish Chaldeans.

Living Godly in Christ Jesus Will Never Be Popular!

> Therefore at that time certain Chaldeans came forward and accused the Jews [literally, chewed them in pieces]. They spoke and said to King Nebuchadnezzar, "O king, live forever! You, O king, have made a decree that everyone who hears the sound of the horn, flute, harp, lyre, and psaltery, in symphony with all kinds of music, shall fall down and worship the gold image; and whoever does not fall down and worship shall be cast into the midst of a burning fiery furnace. There are certain Jews whom you have set over the affairs of the province of Babylon: Shadrach, Meshach, and Abed-Nego; these men, O king, have not paid due regard to you. They do not serve your gods or worship the gold image which you have set up." (Daniel 3:8–12 NKJV)

At the sound of the music, *all* were to bow, and *all* did . . . except the three Hebrews. But how did the Chaldeans know? Someone was peeking! Why was it such a big deal to these Chaldeans that Shadrach, Meshach, and Abednego did not bow? Why is there so much hatred today toward those who live godly? Why, in our world of tolerance, is there so much intolerance toward those who stand with the living God of the Bible? Both the Hebrews that took a stand in ancient Babylon and those who take a stand in our Babylon-like world today will be hated in a culture that is hostile towards God. Our identification with Jesus Christ will always carry a negative response for many. Why?

If God is real, then Jesus Christ is real, then the Bible is real, then sin is real, then judgment is real, then hell is real— all of which is a reality that most refuse to face. Someday they will understand the reality of it all when they kneel before the Eternal Judge, Jesus Christ. But until then, they will continue to show their disdain to those who live godly in our ungodly world. Be prepared for the hurt you will experience through prejudice, jealousy, greed, hatred, and vicious attacks, realizing that "Yea, and all that live godly in Christ Jesus shall suffer persecution" (2 Timothy 3:12).

Prejudice—"There Are Certain Jews"

"Who are these outsiders? They are Jews, not Babylonians. They don't fit in. They are not *one of us*!"

Most fear those who they don't understand. Most fear those who are different in any way. "What if I am wrong and these outsiders are right?" they reason. Prejudiced people are heartless. They live only on the surface and pre-judge someone without even an attempt to get to know their hearts.

Prepare yourself for prejudice. Strong character is almost extinct in our world, and therefore it is viewed as intolerant and inflexible. The best way to deal with prejudice is to put yourself in situations where your antagonists can observe your heart. The meek, kind, generous, and compassionate heart will soften even the most prejudiced of people. Love them to the Lord.

> My brethren, have not the faith of our Lord Jesus Christ, the Lord of glory, with respect of persons. For if there come unto your assembly a man with a gold ring, in goodly apparel, and there come in also a poor man in vile raiment; and ye have respect to him that weareth the gay clothing, and say unto him, Sit thou here in a good place; and say to the poor, Stand thou there, or sit here under my footstool: are ye not then partial in yourselves, and are become judges of evil thoughts? (James 2:1–4)

> If ye fulfil the royal law according to the scripture, Thou shalt love thy neighbor as thyself, ye do well: but if ye have respect to persons, ye commit sin, and are convinced of the law as transgressors. (James 2:8–9)

Jealousy—"Whom You Have Set Over the Affairs of the Province"

"Why do they get to be in charge? They think they are better than us and have even manipulated the king to think the same way. How did they get so popular anyway? Why did King Nebuchadnezzar give them and their friend Daniel such a great promotion over us for more than ten years now? This isn't fair, and we need to do something about it."

Jealousy and insecurity are best friends. A secure leader, confident in his unique God-given gifts, is thankful for what God has given him and refuses to compare or complain about what he does not have. Instead of being upset with the blessings or gifts that God gives to others, he is thankful that God has equipped them to do what he cannot. Jealousy always wants more and will never be satisfied until it is not only obeyed as a king, but worshiped as a god.

When God gives you a position of influence for good, be prepared to face the jealousy of those who want your leadership position and all the perks that go with it—but lack the character and diligence to obtain it.

> Who is wise and understanding among you? Let him show by good conduct that his works are done in the meekness of wisdom. But if you have bitter envy and self-seeking in your hearts, do not boast and lie against the truth. This wisdom does not descend from above, but is earthly, sensual, demonic. For where envy and self-seeking exist, confusion and every evil thing are there. But the wisdom that is from above is first pure, then peaceable, gentle, willing to yield, full of mercy and good fruits, without partiality and without hypocrisy. (James 3:13–17 NKJV)

> For jealousy is the rage of a man: therefore he will not spare in the day of vengeance. (Proverbs 6:34)

Greed—"The Affairs of the Province"

"Until we can get rid of these three Hebrew managers, we will never be able to enjoy the *privileges* of our government jobs. No perks. No bonuses. No tax-funded vacations or extravagant parties. When we are clocked in, we will have to work. We are the rulers in Babylon and should be lavishly treated so. But not as long as Shadrach, Meshach, and Abednego are around."

When you, as a young leader, move into a leadership position, there will be both privileges and temptations. Being treated in a special way, you will begin to believe that you deserve special treatment from everyone. Being surrounded by wealth and privilege could plant seeds of discontent and covetousness in your heart if you are not careful.

God clearly commands, "Thou shall not covet!" (Exodus 20:17). Greed is sneaky, and you don't know it has crept into your heart until it is almost too late. Rather than being thankful for what you do have, you desire more. *More* is so vague it can never be satisfied. *More* always wants more and more and more. Greed is greedy. If you are not careful, what you can get out of life will overshadow how you will give to others. Make sure you understand the devastation and destruction that a greedy, covetous, discontented heart can accomplish.

> He that is greedy of gain troubleth his own house; but he that hateth gifts shall live. (Proverbs 15:27)

> Thou shalt not covet thy neighbor's house, thou shalt not covet thy neighbor's wife, nor his manservant, nor his maidservant, nor his ox, nor his ass, nor any thing that is thy neighbor's. (Exodus 20:17)

Hatred—"That He Should Be Cast Into the Midst of a Burning Fiery Furnace"

"Put them in the fiery furnace. Kill them! We want to see them burn. No, king. Don't give them another chance to bow. Show them who is in charge. Burn them. Burn them alive in the fiery furnace. Make them fry! Kill them!"

Hate hurts. It is one thing to be misunderstood, misjudged, or misspoken, but to literally be hated is hard to take. True hatred is often befriended by cruelty, meanness, spite, and malice. Hatred towards others is motivated by love—a love for self. Hate is a spiritual, fast-growing, incurable cancer of the soul and should be avoided at all costs. Most godly leaders know what it means to be hated.

Even though leaders are personally motivated by a love for God and others, their teaching, preaching, and guidance may be taken as the imposition of unrealistic demands on recipients who turn to hate rather than change. Leaders with lion-like character are no strangers to hate. And no matter how old and how many years of leadership experience you have, hate still hurts. Be prepared to be hated.

> Blessed are ye, when men shall hate you, and when they shall separate you from their company, and shall reproach you, and cast out your name as evil, for the Son of man's sake. Rejoice ye in that day, and leap for joy: for, behold, your reward is great in heaven: for in the like manner did their fathers unto the prophets.

> But I say unto you which hear, Love your enemies, do good to them which hate you, bless them that curse you, and pray for them which despitefully use you. (Luke 6:22–23, 27–28)

> These things I command you, that ye love one another. If the world hate you, ye know that it hated me before it hated you. If ye were of the world, the world would love his own: but because ye are not of the world, but I have chosen you out of the world, therefore the world hateth you. (John 15:17–19)

> Marvel not, my brethren, if the world hate you. (1 John 3:13)

Vicious Attacks—"These Men, O King, Have Not Regarded Thee"

This situation is reminiscent of second-grade tattlers who run to the teacher from the playground saying, "Teacher! Teacher! Do you know what those three boys did at recess? Everyone was supposed to play, . . . and they didn't! They just stood there, and they need to be punished."

In this case, the *teacher* Nebuchadnezzar bought their story and reacted in a fit of rage and fury. He was as childish as the group of Chaldean tattletalers that ran to him.

In our world of blogs, Twitter, Facebook, and an ever-growing demand for Internet presence, those who revel in getting others in trouble and digging up inconsistencies with those that they disagree with will only increase in number, in attacks, and in pitiable character. It is sad that grown men in leadership positions, waste their time attacking others from their pulpits, their newsletters, and their web world.

If you take a stand, you will get attacked. If you do not take a stand, you will get attacked. So all we can do is to walk with God, walk in love, and be prepared to be thrown into the closest fiery furnace around.

> Blessed are ye, when men shall revile you, and persecute you, and shall say all manner of evil against you falsely, for my sake. Rejoice, and be exceeding glad: for great is your reward in heaven: for so persecuted they the prophets which were before you. (Matthew 5:11–12)

> Who [Jesus], when He was reviled, reviled not again; when he suffered, he threatened not; but committed himself to him that judgeth righteously. (1 Peter 2:23)

Living Godly in Christ Jesus Will Always Be Pleasing to God!

> So at that time, when all the people heard the sound of the horn, flute, harp, and lyre, in symphony with all kinds of music, all the people, nations, and languages fell down and worshiped the gold image which King Nebuchadnezzar had set up. (Daniel 3:7 NKJV)

All the people? All the nations? All the languages?

What was the motivating factor for the most educated, the most influential, and even most people—the masses—to bow down and worship Nebuchadnezzar's idol?

Fear! And not just the fear of the flames.

- Fear of being the only one refusing to bow.

- Fear of being different.

- Fear of losing favor with the king.

- Fear of being ridiculed by the crowd.

When fear grips a heart, the knees easily buckle, and before you know it, all are kneeling before those things that everyone else is kneeling before.

The young Hebrews did not bow, because they did not fear. Why? Faith! By *faith* these three "quenched the power of fire." (Hebrews 11:34 ESV). Now faith did not extinguish the flames, it protected them in the midst of the flames. What motivates your heart? Fear or faith?

Why is the fear of rejection so powerful? Fear is much worse than reality. In Hitler's prison camps, torturing prisoners to reveal military secrets profited little. But the threat of torture and pain accomplished great results. The fear of rejection is much worse than rejection. Once you've been rejected you see that life is not over. You can live quite well without the acceptance of those who reject you. You make other friends. You realize that what you experienced was not even close to what our Lord suffered in His rejection.

Why does the fear of ridicule paralyze us? Why is being laughed at so awful? Why should being mocked or bullied be the end of the world? Immaturity laughs at those who are slow mentally. Immaturity ridicules those who are non-athletic. Immaturity makes fun of anyone and everyone that is different—different than what?—different than them! I promise you the Lord was different. I promise you that the three Hebrew musketeers were different.

Fear has a paralyzing effect on all of us. What kind of fear keeps you from sharing Christ with others? What kind of fear keeps you from dressing differently (even modestly) when hanging out with your friends? What kind of fear causes some to take God's name in vain? What kind of fear forces others to say yes to drugs or alcohol? What kind of fear makes many give in to immorality?

Out of the thousands kneeling and bowing before the golden image, three conspicuous, noticeable individuals did not bow. They did not hold a conference; they did not send out a mass mailing; they did not even Facebook their decision; they simply did not bow. Their hearts were made up long before the decree was ever made, and they were not intimidated by their Chaldean peers, their Babylonian king, or the fiery furnace. Bow? No way. They knew God did not want them to bow, so they did not need to defend themselves with the world on why they did not bow. They simply did not bow.

And sorry, but regardless of what *everybody* is saying, *everybody was* not doing it! Hananiah, Mishael, and Azariah were probably about 31 or 32 when they refused to get caught up in the magnificent visual scene or the emotional musical climax of this worship service and bow their foreheads to the ground before this colossus golden idol.

We would love to see such commitment, loyalty, and courage in the hearts of the young leaders we are seeking to raise with similar lion-like character.

> Shadrach [Hananiah], Meshach [Mishael], and Abed-Nego [Azariah]) answered and said to the king, "O Nebuchadnezzar, we have no need to answer you in this matter. If that is the case, our God whom we serve is able to deliver us from the burning fiery furnace, and He will deliver us from your hand, O king. But if not, let it be known to you, O king, that we do not serve your gods, nor will we worship the gold image which you have set up." (Daniel 3:16–18 NKJV)

If That Is the Case . . .

"King Nebuchadnezzar, we know you are furious with us and about to explode with rage. We know that you have everyone watching you: including the most influential, the most successful, and the most educated in your entire kingdom. And since you have made up your mind (by the way, you are not thinking rationally or responsibly trying to get rid of three of your most trusted managers already twice promoted) then we have nothing to say. We have already decided what we are going to do and neither your rage, your influence, nor your death threats will intimidate us."

We Have No Need to Answer You

"We do not need to defend ourselves to you. Nothing we have to say is going to change your mind. You are angry, furious, and we know you will not be reasoned with or listen."

Our God Whom We Serve Is Able to Deliver Us

"Our God is able. He delivered infant Moses from Pharaoh's baby killers. Our God is able. He delivered Joshua from his enemies at Jericho. Our God is able. He delivered Gideon's 300 men from a huge army. Our God is able. He delivered young David from a Philistine giant. Our God is able. He actually created the fire you want to throw us into!"

He Will Deliver Us from Your Hand, O King

"One way or another—either dead or alive; crispy-critters or smoke-free—He will, today, right in front of your eyes show you who is God. And, by the way, king, you can't win on this one. We're already your captive slaves, and to die is to be delivered from Babylon and to move on to our eternal home."

> "But if not [if He only delivers us from you and not from your fiery furnace], let it be known to you, O king, that we do not serve your gods, nor will we worship the gold image which you have set up." (Daniel 3:18 NKJV)

"We will not serve your gods. We want to make it clear to you, O king, . . . we are not going to cave in. We want you to get this, O king, . . . we are not giving in to your threats. We do not want to be misunderstood, O king, . . . we will not budge on this. Let it be known, O king. Never! No way! We are not going to bow!"

Everyone is focused on the flaming furnace. Every people group, every nation, every tongue has turned from the gigantic golden statue, and all are looking at a white-hot furnace with four individuals walking in the midst of the flames. What took months to construct and great sums of money to pay for became worthless in a second—the second three courageous young men took a stand and refused to bow.

If we take a minute and shift our minds back to Daniel, we can see why he chose the close friends he chose. The lion-like character in Hananiah, Azariah, and Mishael is something we wish all our friends possessed. We normally are like those we are around. A close look at Daniel's friends would be a good meditative study for you young leaders to work through.

Friends are important. One of the greatest influences in our lives is friends. God never intended for us to live our lives without friends, and He knew the impact of loneliness when He said, "It is not good that the man should be alone" (Genesis 2:18). Daniel had three friends that we would call best friends. Why did Daniel choose the friends that he had? Daniel could have chosen to be friends with the many Jewish POWs who simply blended in with the crowd. But he didn't. Daniel could have chosen to be friends with the popular Chaldean crowd who were always looking out for themselves. But he didn't. Daniel had the opportunity to be friends with the egotistical King Nebuchadnezzar, who was more interested in being worshiped as a god than being a friend. Daniel instead chose three guys—Hananiah, Mishael, and Azariah—to be his closest companions. What was it about these guys that impressed Daniel to choose such friends?

Daniel's Friends Were Mature Leaders

Even though Daniel's friends were kidnapped POWs who witnessed horrible terror, they refused to focus on their difficult pasts and were known as talented, wise, knowledgeable, understanding, and teachable leaders among their peers.

> Bring some of the children of Israel . . . young men in
> whom there was no blemish, but good-looking, gifted in all
> wisdom, possessing knowledge and quick to understand,
> who had ability to serve in the king's palace, and whom they

might teach the language and literature of the Chaldeans. (Daniel 1:3–4 NKJV)

Daniel's friends were leaders and not losers. They studied! They worked hard! Daniel chose friends who were going somewhere in life because he wanted to do the same. Losers lose because they have no direction, no drive, and no desire to please anyone but themselves.

- Are your friends leaders or losers?

- Do your friends draw you closer to the Lord or drive you farther away from the Lord?

- What kind of leader are you?

- In what way have you helped or encouraged one of your friends in his or her walk with the Lord during this past school year?

Daniel's Friends Were Gifted by God

His friends were gifted in unique ways and were willing to use those gifts to fulfill God's plan for their lives.

As for these four young men, God gave them knowledge and skill in all literature and wisdom; and Daniel had understanding in all visions and dreams. (Daniel 1:17 NKJV)

In what unique way has God gifted you? How do you and your friends encourage each other to perfect those God-given gifts and use them to honor God? Those of you gifted in music, do you practice consistently? Those of you gifted in working with people, have you set some goals to work at camps, children's ministries, or summer mission teams?

Daniel's Friends Stood Out Above Their Peers

Because of God's work in their lives, they appeared ten times better than their peers.

Then the king interviewed them, and among them all none was found like Daniel, Hananiah, Mishael, and Azariah; therefore they served before the king. And in all matters of wisdom and understanding about which the king examined them, he found them ten times better than all the magicians and astrologers who were in all his realm. (Daniel 1:19–20 NKJV)

Never settle for mediocrity. Never be satisfied with boring. Don't waste your life going with the flow, but choose friends that will go against the flow with you. How do your friends energize you to live with a spirit of excellence that *pole vaults* you over the *whatever lifestyle* of most teens?

Daniel's Friends Knew How to Pray

They knew how to fervently seek God in prayer and ask for answers.

So Daniel went in and asked the king to give him time, that he might tell the king the interpretation. Then Daniel went to his house, and made the decision known to Hananiah, Mishael, and Azariah, his companions, that they might seek mercies from the God of heaven concerning this secret, so that Daniel and his companions might not perish with the rest of the wise men of Babylon. Then the secret was revealed to Daniel in a night vision. So Daniel blessed the God of heaven. (Daniel 2:16–19 NKJV)

Don't be afraid to ask yourself some hard questions.

- Do you pray with your friends?
- Do you pray for your friends?
- Do you ever get together at a friend's homes or at a coffee shop and share prayer requests with each other?
- Would you like to have a friend prays for you?

Daniel shared his request with his companions that they might seek mercies from the God of heaven. Anyone who has friends that know how to seek God in prayer is a truly blessed individual.

Daniel and His Friends Were a Team

They stuck together through the good and the bad times.

Then the king promoted Daniel and gave him many great gifts; and he made him ruler over the whole province of Babylon, and chief administrator over all the wise men of Babylon. Also Daniel petitioned the king, and he set Shadrach, Meshach, and Abed-Nego over the affairs of the province of Babylon; but Daniel sat in the gate of the king. (Daniel 2:48–49 NKJV)

Loyalty is a lost art today. It doesn't seem to take much for friends to get mad at each other and begin attacking each other. When you fall, true friends will pick you up and never kick you while you are down.

Two are better than one; because they have a good reward for their labour. For if they fall, the one will lift up his fellow: but woe to him that is alone when he falleth; for he hath not another to help him up. (Ecclesiastes 4:9–11)

Daniel's Friends Did Not Fear Death

Because they were men of purpose and men of prayer, they were able to stand against the ultimate of all fears— death. Regardless of the pressure, they had already determined that they would never serve the Babylonian gods.

Shadrach, Meshach, and Abednego, answered and said to the king, O Nebuchadnezzar, we are not careful to answer thee in this matter. [We do not need to defend ourselves in this.] If it be so, our God whom we serve is able to deliver us from the burning fiery furnace, and He will deliver us out of thine hand, O king. But if not, be it known unto thee, O king that we will not serve thy gods, nor worship the golden image which thou hast set up. (Daniel 3:16–18)

King Nebuchadnezzar did not just want to be obeyed, he wanted to be worshiped! This was a declaration of spiritual warfare. Hananiah, Mishael, and Azariah made three statements which screamed out their confidence with conviction.

1. "Our God whom we serve is able."

2. "He will deliver us out of thine hand."

3. "But if not, be it known unto thee, O king that we will not serve thy gods!"

Daniel's Friends Had an Impact on Their Ungodly Society
Even their unbelieving acquaintances knew that they trusted their God, obeyed their God, and were willing to die rather than serve or worship any other god except the one true God.

> Then Nebuchadnezzar spake, and said, Blessed be the God of Shadrach, Meshach, and Abednego, who hath sent his angel, and delivered his servants that trusted in him, and have changed the king's word, and yielded their bodies, that they might not serve nor worship any god, except their own God. (Daniel 3:28)

Out of the thousands kneeling and bowing before the golden image, three conspicuous, noticeable, obvious individuals did not bow. Their hearts were made up long before the decree was made, and they were not intimidated by their Chaldean peers, their Babylonian king, or their fiery furnace. Bow? No way. Could you make same choice?

Daniel's Friends Were Never Accepted
No, Daniel and his friends were never accepted, but they were respected and honored.

> Then the king promoted Shadrach, Meshach, and Abednego, in the province of Babylon. (Daniel 3:30)

Shadrach, Meshach, and Abednego were the Tim Tebows of their day. They gave hope and courage to hundreds of other persecuted Jewish teens who were *take-a-stand wannabees*. Will you become the kind of friend that Daniel would choose if he were alive today?

Push Pause

Couldn't Shadrach, Meshach, and Abednego have just pretended to bow down on the outside—but not on the inside?

Couldn't Daniel have just prayed with the windows shut or in his office?

Virtual reality is a part of our high-tech world and becoming more real every day. Virtual reality is virtually real!

Virtual obedience has become a part of our Christian world, and far too many of us are fine tuning and mastering this art. Virtual obedience looks like the real thing, so much so that you can hardly discern if your obedience is real or not. We attend church, but do we truly worship? We read our Bibles, but do we internalize its message? We pray, or at least verbalize the words *forgive me* and *give me*, but do we connect with God through "effectual fervency"? We give our tithes, but out of devotion or duty? We try to stay away from visible worldliness, but is it because of our fear of the consequences or embarrassment or our love for the Lord?

Think about Andrew Tuplin's thoughts below as he deals with the morality of virtual reality in his article posted on *Adbusters*.

Virtual reality is becoming more prominent and dangerous every day. You can now assume a second identity online, marry a virtual wife, and even have virtual children. You can act as a Russian terrorist and run through airports killing innocent civilians. You can rob banks, gamble, hustle drugs, or shoot people all in the name of fun. These are just a few of the developments of the ever growing, emotionally degrading, and morally demeaning virtual reality mediums.

> By putting choice and consequence in closed virtual worlds where we can kill without harming others or facing punishment ourselves, we are forced to reconsider the case for moral behavior. . . . videogames such as *Grand Theft Auto IV* and online communities such as *Second Life*, invite an increasingly large percentage of society to participate in fantasy worlds where we are invited to experience life without rules—to be the bad guy or the sexual deviant. . . . What Jesus teaches is that God is concerned not only with what plays out in the physical world of actions (reality),

but also with what takes place in the **virtual world of our minds**.[2] [author's emphasis]

Push Play

Then Nebuchadnezzar was full of fury and the expression on his face changed toward Shadrach, Meshach, and Abed-nego [Hananiah, Mishael and Azariah]. He spoke and commanded that they heat the furnace seven times more than it was usually heated. And he commanded certain mighty men of valor who were in his army to bind Shadrach, Meshach, and Abed-nego, and cast them into the burning fiery furnace. Then these men were bound in their coats, their trousers, their turbans, and their other garments, and were cast into the midst of the burning fiery furnace [right on top of the burning coals]. Therefore, because the king's command was urgent, and the furnace exceedingly hot, the flame of the fire killed those men who took up [to top of the blast furnace] Shadrach, Meshach, and Abed-Nego. And these three men, Shadrach, Meshach, and Abed-Nego, fell down bound into the midst of the burning fiery furnace. (Daniel 3:19–23 NKJV)

Warren Wiersbe in his *Bible Exposition Commentary of the Old Testament* states:

The furnace was used for smelting ore. It had a large opening at the top through which fuel and vessels full of ore could be placed into the fire, and there was a door at the bottom through which the metal was taken out. An opening in a wall enabled the smelters to check on the progress of their work, and through holes in the wall they could use bellows to make the fire blaze even more. The unit was large enough to walk around in it. It was into this furnace that Nebuchadnezzar cast the three faithful Jews, fully clothed and bound. It seemed like certain death for the men who refused to obey the king.[3]

The metal-smelting furnace was hot. The fire had to be at least 1,850 degrees Fahrenheit to melt gold, 1,700 degrees to melt silver, 1,200 degrees to melt bronze, 2,000 degrees to melt cast iron, and 2,800 to melt iron. Again, to melt gold the fire had to be at least 1,850 degrees, but only 212 degrees Fahrenheit to boil water. Since our bodies are made mostly of water, by the time our body temperature reached 212 degrees Fahrenheit our water would turn to steam and we would be gone. Bound, with no chance to run away when the soldiers died, the Hebrews were thrown into the furnace. As the ropes that bound them burned off, they stood up and walked around without even being singed by the flames. As life evaporated (literally *sucked from*) out of the soldiers, I am sure the three thought their lives were over and they would soon be in the presence of the Lord. Well, their lives were not over, but they were in the presence of the Lord. As they stood and began to walk, a fourth person walked with them. Was it an angel? Was it our Lord Jesus Himself? For the pagan king, who knew nothing of the second person of the Trinity, he simply meant that the fourth was a supernatural being likened as a very "son of God"—the Lord Jesus Christ (Christophany) came, protected them, walked with them, and comforted them.

Hananiah, Mishael, and Azariah (Shadrach, Meshach, and Abednego) were not the only ones in history to be persecuted with fire. Many believers suffered in Nero's burning of Rome as he used them as human torches to light his gardens. How many reformers tied to stakes, praised God as the flames wrapped around their bodies and took their lives. We can only hope that many suffocated from the smoke before the flames tortured their bodies.

> Then King Nebuchadnezzar was astonished; and he rose in haste and spoke, saying to his counselors, "Did we not cast three men bound into the midst of the fire?" They answered and said to the king, "True, O king." "Look!" he answered, "I see four men loose, walking in the midst of the fire; and they

are not hurt, and the form of the fourth is like the Son of God." (Daniel 3:24–25 NKJV)

What was Nebuchadnezzar's response when he saw that he was wrong and God was right? Even public figures are private souls who are accountable to God.

Nebuchadnezzar was *astonished*. He rose in haste. He sought counsel. He couldn't believe his eyes. He went near the furnace and felt the heat that killed his soldiers.

Nebuchadnezzar was *admonished*. He admitted that Jehovah was the Most High God and recognized God's deliverance of His servants who refused to serve or worship any god except their own God. How did they do this? They had confidence in the power of God. They trusted in Him And refused to compromise or yield to the king—"frustrated the king's word" (Daniel 3:28). They had peace with the will of God. They were willing to be delivered. They were willing to die—"yielded their bodies" (Daniel 3:28).

King Nebuchadnezzar saw a visual example of Isaiah's prophecy.

> "Fear not, for I have redeemed you; I have called you by your name; You are Mine. When you pass through the waters, I will be with you; and through the rivers, they shall not overflow you. When you walk through the fire, you shall not be burned, nor shall the flame scorch you. For I am the Lord your God, the Holy One of Israel, your Savior . . . you were precious in My sight, You have been honored, and I have loved you." (Isaiah 43:1–4 NKJV)

Shadrach, Meshach, and Abednego gave hope and courage to hundreds of other persecuted Jewish teens. As we move toward the end of the age, the furnace of opposition will be heated seven times hotter and the pressure to conform will become stronger and stronger. It will take a great deal of grace, prayer, courage, and faith for God's people to stand tall for Christ while others are bowing the knee to the gods of this world. The book of Daniel is a great source of encouragement, because it reminds us that God cares for His people and honors them when they are true to Him.

Them that honour me I will honour. (1 Samuel 2:30)

No matter how despotic the world's rulers become or how hot they stoke the furnace, God will be with His people in the furnace and will ultimately defeat their enemies and establish His kingdom. When you choose to love your Lord, when you choose to be loyal to your Lord, along with your choice comes the loneliness of leadership. You may feel lonely, but you will never be truly alone.

"Look!" the king answered, "I see four men loose, walking in the midst of the fire; and they are not hurt, and the form of the fourth is like the Son of God."

Yea, and all that will live godly in Christ Jesus shall suffer persecution. (2 Timothy 3:12)

REFUSE TO LIVE A GODLESS LIFE

DANIEL 5:1–31

Belshazzar Learned That Life Is No Party

His invincibility was an illusion. His indestructible fortress was a mirage. His rash choice to mock the God of heaven and live a godless life was but one small laugh at his life's party. Life is not a party, and for those who think it is, you had better keep your eyes on the wall.

As a young leader, you need to remember that sin has consequences. You can choose your sin, but you cannot choose the consequences of your sin. There are certain games that, if played, you will lose. God is faithful to forgive, but forgiveness does not necessarily mean the removal of the consequences of the sin forgiven.

Daniel served under King Belshazzar who was the grandson of King Nebuchadnezzar. A slow read through Daniel 5:1–31 gives a good picture of Belshazzar's infamous feast. In one short chapter of thirty-one verses we can see Belshazzar's life unfold in a dramatic three-act play entitled "Proverbs 29:1." The subtitle is "He, that being often reproved hardeneth his neck, shall suddenly be destroyed and that without remedy." The lessons taught in this drama are vitally important for you to learn, understand, and use as red flags in your choice of entertainment and friends.

Act One: I Warned You—*"he being often reproved"*

Act Two: You Ignored Me—*"hardens his neck"*

Act Three: Now, Your Party Is Over—*will be destroyed*

Belshazzar the King Made a Great Feast to a Thousand of His Lords . . .

Who is Belshazzar? How and when did he come to rule? Inspirational commentator Charles Swindoll in *Daniel: God's Pattern for the Future* colorfully describes the events from King Nebuchadnezzar's death to his grandson, Belshazzar's reign.

> In the heavily fortified city, Belshazzar lounged comfortably on his velvet-covered throne. No invader had been able to storm the city. Babylon was considered impregnable. . . . Safe within the city, Belshazzar made light of the news. What harm could Cyrus' spears and arrows do against Babylon's 87-foot wide, massive stone walls and impassable moat? When Cyrus besieged the city, Belshazzar still just shrugged his shoulders. There was a twenty-year supply of food in the huge granaries. Cyrus and his men would run out of provisions long before Belshazzar and his people.
>
> So the arrogant king scoffed at Cyrus' siege and conceived the perfect way to show how confident of victory he was—he threw a party.[1]

Belshazzar's party could have been an extravagant feast of thanksgiving to the Creator God who gave to this Babylonian leader all that he had. The music could have been based on pageantry and grandeur rather than lust and licentiousness. The delicacies and fine foods could have been enjoyed knowing that the God who makes the sun to rise and the rains to fall gave such to enjoy. The dancing could have been joyous and not sensual. The laughter and merriment could have been prompted by God's goodness rather than fleshly covetousness. The beauty of the décor could have been a glimpse of what heaven will be like rather than a pronouncement of what this selfish king lavishly enjoyed. It is not sin to party. It all depends on why you choose to party.

> Belshazzar . . . drank wine before the thousand. Belshazzar, whiles he tasted the wine, commanded to bring the golden and silver vessels which his [grand]father Nebuchadnezzar had taken out of the temple which was in Jerusalem; that the king, and his princes, his wives, and his concubines, might drink therein. Then they brought the golden vessels that were taken out of the temple of the house of God which was at Jerusalem; and the king, and his princes, his wives, and his concubines, drank in them. They drank wine, and praised the gods of gold, and of silver, of brass, of iron, of wood, and of stone. (Daniel 5:1–3)

Belshazzar was not only drunk with wine, he was drunk with pride. In his arrogance he sought to prove to his 1000 puppet lords that he was greater than Cyrus, greater than Nebuchadnezzar, greater than Daniel, and even greater than Daniel's so-called *living* God. With brazen blasphemy he sent for the pure gold drinking vessels that his grandfather Nebuchadnezzar had taken from the holy temple of Jerusalem and displayed as sacred treasures in Babylon. Filling them with wine he proposed a toast to himself and to his gods to show how invincible he was before both the king of Persia and the King of Heaven. Where there was no restraint to the lowest vices of self-indulgence, there was no realization that all men will kneel before God. Foolish reveling is a result of foolish thinking. Before anyone feels he has the liberty to be licentious, he has already ignored or even despised God's ultimate authority over his life.

There were many foreign gods that Belshazzar could have chosen to mock. His grandfather Nebuchadnezzar and father Nabonidus had conquered many cities and peoples, and he sat in his invincible castle city of Babylon impervious to attack or defeat. Why did he choose a battle with the Hebrew God? Belshazzar pretended to be a sovereign ruler whose word was the final law but all the while knew that there was a true, living, heavenly sovereign ruler whose word had already been expressed and would overrule anything Belshazzar said. Belshazzar was seeking to attack and discredit the very words of God. He wouldn't believe them and wouldn't accept them, so he sought to discredit and destroy them. His plan failed.

He may have wanted to put to rest once and for all the interpretation of King Nebuchadnezzar's great dream recorded in Daniel 2 of the statue made of gold, silver, bronze, iron, and clay that spoke of an inferior nation destroying his kingdom.

He may have wanted to silence the voice of the wisest man in the kingdom, a man not accepted but respected by many, a man of integrity who refused the brainwashing techniques of the Babylonian courtiers and boldly told the great King Nebuchadnezzar that because of his pride and refusal to give God His deserved honor he would become like a wild animal. He would go insane. This famous story in Babylon was an embarrassment to his kingly arrogance.

> They shall drive you from men, your dwelling shall be with the beasts of the field, and they shall make you eat grass like oxen. They shall wet you with the dew of heaven, and seven times shall pass over you, **till you know that the Most High rules in the kingdom of men, and gives it to whomever He chooses.** (Daniel 4:25 NKJV)

He may have wanted to discredit one of Israel's famous and fear-inducing prophets named Jeremiah who in a carefully detailed way foretold the fall of Babylon. Spurgeon speculates that Daniel must have read, studied, meditated on, and wept over this prophecy of Jeremiah. Put yourself in Daniel's sandals and think about these prophetic words that God spoke through the prophet Jeremiah:

> The word that the Lord spoke against Babylon and against the land of the Chaldeans by Jeremiah the prophet. "Declare

among the nations, proclaim, and set up a standard; proclaim—do not conceal it—say, 'Babylon is taken, Bel is shamed. Merodach is broken in pieces; her idols are humiliated, her images are broken in pieces.' For out of the north a nation comes up against her, which shall make her land desolate, and no one shall dwell therein. They shall move, they shall depart, both man and beast." (Jeremiah 50:1–3 NKJV)

Make bright the arrows; gather the shields: the Lord hath raised up the spirit of the kings of the Medes: for his device is against Babylon, to destroy it; because it is the vengeance of the Lord, the vengeance of His temple. (Jeremiah 51:11)

And I will make drunk her princes, and her wise men, her captains, and her rulers, and her mighty men: and they shall sleep a perpetual sleep, and not wake, saith the King, whose name is the Lord of hosts. (Jeremiah 51:57)

In the same hour came forth fingers of a man's hand, and wrote over against the candlestick upon the plaister of the wall of the king's palace: and the king saw the part of the hand that wrote. (Daniel 5:5)

Invincible, proud, blasphemous Belshazzar is shaken to his core right in the middle of his party. He had spent hours (and huge amounts of money) to show that he was supreme. The real Belshazzar was revealed the second God's hand began writing on the wall—the hand of the same God they were mocking.

When God's hand started writing on the wall, what good were Belshazzar's gods to him then? He had trusted in gods of wood that would rot and decay, gods of iron that would rust, gods of silver and brass that would tarnish, gods of stone, that would remain as "dumb as rocks," and gods of gold. He could not buy his way out of this one. His pretend gods were powerless, and he was now accountable to the God of all gods, the one true living God.

> Then the king's countenance was changed, and his thoughts
> troubled him, so that the joints of his loins were loosed, and
> his knees smote one against another. (Daniel 5:6)

Belshazzar could not read what was written on the wall.
Why was he so shaken? Can you imagine all that went
through his troubled mind that night? Was it the drunkenness? The sensual dancers? The immorality? The haughty
lies? The idolatry? The crass and vulgar jesting? The mocking
of God's people and their God by desecrating the cups taken
from their holy temple? Why was he so scared?

The Terror of a Guilty Conscience

A guilty conscience is a terrifying thing. King Belshazzar
was visibly changed by the presence of God's hand. What
physically happened to Belshazzar is described a number of
different ways as seen in the various translations of Daniel 5:6.

> Then the king's countenance was changed, and his thoughts
> troubled him, so that the joints of his loins were loosed, and
> his knees smote one against another. (KJV)

> Then the king's countenance changed, and his thoughts
> troubled him, so that the joints of his hips were loosened
> and his knees knocked against each other. (NKJV)

> His face turned pale and he was so frightened that his legs
> became weak and his knees were knocking. (NIV)

> Then the king's color changed, and his thoughts alarmed
> him; his limbs gave way, and his knees knocked together.
> (ESV)

Why? If he had license to do what he wanted to do, why?
If he was the king with no one to answer to, why? If he dis-
dained and despised God so, why? If he thought God was so
weak, why? Because he knew his choice to live a life without
God did not mean that God did not exist and would not
hold him accountable someday. Why? He knew he was guilty
before a holy God!

> Are you in an emotional battle because of guilt? Is your guilt a loving instrument of God used to convict, correct, and conform your character or do you battle feelings of shame and condemnation when guilt strikes a blow to your heart? True guilt is your friend—a godly companion who whispers truth and motivates you to repent and be free. But false guilt is a relentless foe. It is the enemy within that encourages not godly, but superficial sorrow that brings death! [2]

It is one thing to live on a fat-free, sodium-free, sugar-free, and even gluten-free diet. It is another thing to live a guilt-free life.

> The king cried aloud to bring in the astrologers, the Chaldeans, and the soothsayers. And the king spake, and said to the wise men of Babylon, Whosoever shall read this writing, and shew me the interpretation thereof, shall be clothed with scarlet, and have a chain of gold about his neck, and shall be the third ruler in the kingdom. Then came in all the king's wise men: but they could not read the writing, nor make known to the king the interpretation thereof. Then was king Belshazzar greatly troubled, and his countenance was changed in him, and his lords were astonied. (Daniel 5:7–9)

Belshazzar lost it. He "cried aloud!" The king screamed in hysteria for someone to get some help. For over twenty years he had lived a completely godless life by choosing to reject and even scorn the only true, living God.

He first cried to the ***astrologers***. These were the enchanters, the magicians. This was not a magic show. Even with their occult connections they were helpless. Their magic tricks and illusions were not going to appease this king or this crowd.

He then cried to the ***Chaldeans***. Certainly these priests of the gods of the Babylonians could help here. Where is the power of Marduk? What about Bel-Merodach? Where is the Dragon or Bel? Come on guys, we have sacrificed to these gods so many times, where are they when we need them?

He finally cried to the **soothsayers**. These were the fortune tellers. Some believed that the stars and the planets controlled their destiny. Others dug deep into the recesses of the demonic world to spout Satan's lies. Again, as they looked at the handwriting on the wall, they were not only helpless, they were hopeless and would die with the other pretenders.

You had better be careful where you look for answers to life. Where you look for your power and protection during the good times is where you will look when the tragedies come.

Let Daniel Be Called

> Now the queen, by reason of the words of the king and his lords, came into the banquet house: and the queen spake and said, O king, live forever: let not thy thoughts trouble thee, nor let thy countenance be changed: there is a man in thy kingdom, in whom is the spirit of the holy gods; and in the days of thy father light and understanding and wisdom, like the wisdom of the gods, was found in him; whom the king Nebuchadnezzar thy father, the king, I say, thy father, made master of the magicians, astrologers, Chaldeans, and soothsayers; forasmuch as an excellent spirit, and knowledge, and understanding, interpreting of dreams, and shewing of hard sentences, and dissolving of doubts, were found in the same Daniel, whom the king named Belteshazzar: **now let Daniel be called**, and he will shew the interpretation. (Daniel 5:10–12)

Daniel is still known by his Hebrew name over seventy years after coming to Babylon. Here was a solid oak tree standing before a weeping willow of a king. Daniel's roots were dug deep into a living God while Belshazzar chose to live without that God. Daniel is a great teacher. Before he tells *what* was written on the wall, he gives them some background and tells them *why* it was written. He also emphasizes the fact that Belshazzar knew better and had absolutely no excuse before God. Men may blaspheme God with their puny lives today, but when they stand before His final words of judgment, there will be nothing they can say. Their parties will be over.

> Then was Daniel brought in before the king. And the king spake and said unto Daniel, Art thou that Daniel, which art of the children of the captivity of Judah, whom the king my father brought out of Jewry? I have even heard of thee, that the spirit of the gods is in thee, and that light and under- standing and excellent wisdom is found in thee. And now the wise men, the astrologers, have been brought in before me, that they should read this writing, and make known unto me the interpretation thereof: but they could not shew the interpretation of the thing: and I have heard of thee that thou canst make interpretations, and dissolve doubts: now if thou canst read the writing, and make known to me the interpretation thereof, thou shalt be clothed with scarlet, and have a chain of gold about thy neck, and shalt be the third ruler in the kingdom. (Daniel 5:13–16)

Belshazzar's pride is seen in the way he mockingly wel- comed elderly Daniel. Looking down his royal nose at this old, wasted, Jewish exile he offered him what he had person- ally given his life for. Stuff! It is as if a tiny pebble seeks to impress a huge bolder. Belshazzar offered a scarlet robe, a necklace of gold, and a few minutes of popularity. The fool- ishness of such riches and power paled in comparison with the deep rooted integrity that Daniel possessed from walking with God for decades. How foolish Belshazzar's offer must have been to Daniel.

> For what profit is it to a man if he gains the whole world, and loses his own soul? Or what will a man give in exchange for his soul? For the Son of Man will come in the glory of His Father with His angels, and then He will reward each accord- ing to his works. (Matthew 16:26–27)

When finally caught and confronted, Belshazzar tried to appease God and God's man with a gold necklace and a purple robe, but God's divine creed had been written. And if you think the law of the Medes and Persians was binding, try to reverse God's words of judgment or eternal judgment.

> Then Daniel answered and said before the king, Let thy gifts be to thyself, and give thy rewards to another; [No thank you. Even as an exiled slave I don't need your trinkets to be happy. All your extravagant riches will do you no good now, and you cannot buy your way out of this one.] yet I will read the writing unto the king, and make known to him the interpretation. O thou king, the most high God gave Nebuchadnezzar thy father a kingdom, and majesty, and glory, and honour: and for the majesty that He gave him, all people, nations, and languages, trembled and feared before him: whom he would he slew; and whom he would he kept alive; and whom he would he set up; and whom he would he put down. (Daniel 5:17–22)

If Daniel was confronting Belshazzar today, it might have sounded something like this.

"You Belshazzar don't even begin to compare with your grandfather Nebuchadnezzar. He had a kingdom of his own. He had it all! The only reason you are where you are is because your daddy needed someone to watch over Babylon. Majesty, glory, and honor! Yours is all pretend. The only way you can get your people to honor you is to throw your own party and try to wow them with the allowance your daddy Nabonidus lets you have each week. You think you are better than Nebuchadnezzar? The people in his kingdom feared and trembled before him, and your royal subjects laugh at you and will actually rejoice when your kingdom is taken away from you. And if you don't remember what God did to humble Nebuchadnezzar? Let me remind you.

> But when his heart was lifted up, and his spirit was hardened in pride, he was deposed from his kingly throne, and they took his glory from him. Then he was driven from the sons of men, his heart was made like the beasts, and his dwelling was with the wild donkeys. They fed him with grass like oxen, and his body was wet with the dew of heaven, till he

knew that the Most High God rules in the kingdom of men, and appoints over it whomsoever He chooses.

But you his son, Belshazzar, have not humbled your heart, although you knew all this. [You didn't forget, you only pretended to forget. You were not ignorant of almighty God's ultimate authority, you simply ignored it!] And you have lifted yourself up against the Lord of heaven. They have brought the vessels of His house before you, and you, and your lords, your wives and your concubines, have drunk wine from them. And you have praised the gods of silver and gold, bronze and iron, wood and stone, which do not see or hear or know; and the God who holds your breath in His hand, [You breathe without thinking. But whenever God decides that He does not want you to breathe any longer—your life is over.] and owns all your ways, you have not glorified: [You exalted yourself above God! You made yourself more important than God in your own eyes. You made fun of God's holy temple, God's chosen people, and God Himself. You are as empty as the make-believe gods you worship—just as blind, just as dumb, and just as stupid. The very breath that God gives you, you have used to curse Him. And by the way, that hand of God—that holds your life and breath— is writing on your wall. Belshazzar, I hope you enjoyed your party, because it is about over, and you will have eternity—forever and forever and forever—in misery and pain remembering everything you have pretended to forget.] (Daniel 5:20–23 NKJV)

I am sure that Belshazzar knew what Daniel told Nebuchadnezzar about each of the kingdoms that would follow his (the Babylonians, the Medes and Persians, the Macedonians, the Romans). When God was finished with each kingdom, there was nothing left. Like the wind blows away worthless chaff, nothing.

Although immorality has stolen the love of many away from God and expressed itself in a love for self, this is not what Daniel attacked. Perversions are pervasive in our permissive world. If you want to understand God's concern in this area, meditate on 1 Thessalonians 4, Romans 1, Ephesians 5, and Proverbs 4–7.

Although drunkenness is condemned by God, this is not what Daniel attacked. Solomon clearly teaches the negative consequences of soaking your rational thinking in booze. The old story is told of a man who had the choice of three sins he could commit—drunkenness, adultery, or murder. He chose drunkenness because it did not seem as bad as adultery or murder. But while he was intoxicated he committed both the others, and thus was guilty of all three.

Although blasphemy was listed in Belshazzar's entertainment plan, this is not what Daniel dealt with. When a man refuses to acknowledge God or glorify God, it is just a matter of time before he begins to belittle God, His Word, and His people. It is not long before the belittling transforms into blasphemy.

> Then was the part of the hand sent from him; and this writing was written. And this is the writing that was written, MENE, MENE, TEKEL, UPHARSIN. This is the interpretation of the thing: MENE; God hath numbered thy kingdom, and finished it. TEKEL; Thou art weighed in the balances, and art found wanting. PERES; Thy kingdom is divided, and given to the Medes and Persians. (Daniel 5:24–28)

God crashed Belshazzar's party with a very important text.

- *Mene, Mene*—counted (it is doubled for emphasis)
  All of our days are numbered before we stand before God.

- *Tekel*—weighed or assessed in the scale of God's impeccable judgment
  Either you are weighed in the balances and found wanting, or you are weighed in the balances and found complete in Christ.

- *Upharsin*—the *u* means *and* / *pharsin* is plural for *peres* which means divided (to the Medes and the Persians)
  There are consequences to all of our choices.

Daniel overlooked great displays of external wickedness to condemn the true heart issue. We may have never hosted a party like Belshazzar's with every form of sin, wickedness, and vice imaginable, but our hearts could mirror Belshazzar's heart if we are not careful.

> Then commanded Belshazzar, and they clothed Daniel with scarlet, and put a chain of gold about his neck, and made a proclamation concerning him, that he should be the third ruler in the kingdom. In that night was Belshazzar the king of the Chaldeans slain. And Darius the Median took the kingdom, being about threescore and two years old. (Daniel 5:29–31)

After Daniel interpreted God's written text on the wall, it was almost as if Belshazzar did not believe it. He offered the robe and the necklace and acted as if all was going to stay the same. He did not realize that his party was almost over. It sounded like it was the end of a 20-plus year party for Belshazzar. But sad to say, his life is not over, and he will be reminded of his godless choices, his godless life, and his godless palace as he continues to live forever in a godless eternity.

He played throughout his life, and now he will pay throughout his eternity. Don't let pride blur your ability to see what you should be taking seriously in life. Taking serious things lightly was Belshazzar's deadly mistake. His invincibility was an illusion. His indestructible fortress was a mirage. Life is not a party . . . and for those of who think it is, you had better keep your eyes on the wall.

That Very Night

> One ancient account alleged that Persia's General Ugbaru had troops dig a trench to divert and thus lower the waters of the Euphrates River; since the river flowed through the city of Babylon, the lowered water enabled besiegers to unexpectedly invade via the waterway under the thick walls and reach the palace before the city was aware. The end then came quickly on October 16, BC 539.[3]

Both King Nebuchadnezzar and his grandson, King Belshazzar egotistically viewed themselves as gods—gods who were even greater than the living God of Israel. Ezekiel, who lived during Daniel's time in Babylon, described a similar king from the city of Tyre who lived and died much like King Belshazzar. Isaiah, who lived about 200 years before Daniel and Ezekiel, seems to be describing a very similar situation to the king of Tyre and the king of Babylon. I trust that Isaiah's warning and Ezekiel's prophecy would never be true of your life or of the lives of your children.

The word of the Lord came to me again, saying, "Son of man, say to the prince of Tyre, 'Thus says the Lord God:

"Because your heart is lifted up, and you say, 'I am a god, I sit in the seat of gods, in the midst of the seas,' yet you are a man, and not a god, though you set your heart as the heart of a god (Behold, [in your mind] you are wiser than Daniel! There is no secret that can be hidden from you! With your wisdom and your understanding you have gained riches for yourself, and gathered gold and silver into your treasuries; by your great wisdom in trade you have increased your riches, and your heart is lifted up because of your riches),"

'Therefore thus says the Lord God:

"Because you have set your heart as the heart of a god, behold, therefore, I will bring strangers against you, the most terrible of the nations; and they shall draw their swords against the beauty of your wisdom, and defile your splendor. They shall throw you down into the Pit, and you shall die the death of the slain In the midst of the seas. "Will you still say before him who slays you, 'I am a god'? But you shall be a man, and not a god, in the hand of him who slays you. You shall die the death of the uncircumcised by the hand of aliens;

for I have spoken," says the Lord God.' " (Ezekiel 28:1–10 NKJV)

"For you have trusted in your wickedness; you have said, 'No one sees me'; your wisdom and your knowledge have warped you; and you have said in your heart, 'I am, and there is no one else besides me.' Therefore evil shall come upon you; you shall not know from where it arises. And trouble shall fall upon you; you will not be able to put it off. And desolation shall come upon you suddenly, which you shall not know.

"Stand now with your enchantments and the multitude of your sorceries, in which you have labored from your youth—perhaps you will be able to profit, perhaps you will prevail. You are wearied in the multitude of your counsels; let now the astrologers, the stargazers, and the monthly prognosticators stand up and save you from what shall come upon you. Behold, they shall be as stubble, the fire shall burn them; they shall not deliver themselves from the power of the flame; it shall not be a coal to be warmed by, nor a fire to sit before! Thus shall they be to you with whom you have labored, your merchants from your youth; they shall wander each one to his quarter. No one shall save you." (Isaiah 47:10–15 NKJV)

Now we have heard the story.

The life of Belshazzar can be described in one word—god-less. This is not a story of hope, but of judgment. Belshazzar had his opportunities: he had a mother who seemingly still feared God and trusted the words of God's man; he had a grandfather whose story of selfishness and pride should have been a solemn warning; he had the writings of Isaiah and Ezekiel to convict his heart; and he had Daniel—but refused to get counsel from him. He did everything to stay as far away from God as he could. He was godless.

Maybe he forgot? No, these men don't forget; they act like they have forgotten, but they don't forget. How do I know? At the zenith of his arrogance, he asked for the gold drinking vessels from the temple of Jerusalem, the temple of the living God, to show his superiority over such an adored God. Belshazzar was a godless man.

Never determine a man's success by the size of his parties or the number of his friends. Don't honor anyone because he has thousands of fans and millions of dollars. What will his friends and wealth do for him when he enters a godless eternity? You don't want to be part of that party.

PART THREE

14 LAWS OF COURAGEOUS LEADERSHIP

Show-and-Tell

We need more Daniels and Danielles in our world today. In regards to integrity, character, and fearlessness, our world is almost bankrupt.

Most of us have heard more about the lions' den than we have about Daniel. There are 153 verses about Daniel's life before he was dropped into the den of lions, but absolutely zero describing what went on in the lions' den where God miraculously shut the lions' mouths. Let's not miss God's eighty-plus year miracle that He performed in Daniel's life. As Daniel lovingly and loyally yielded to God, God enabled him with grace-filled qualities that were foundational for his excellent spirit and lion-like character.

Life would be so much easier if character came in capsule form or was the prime ingredient in a power drink. But character must be both taught and caught.

Do you remember show-and-tell days at your elementary school? There was no stopping the bugs, spiders, bikes, and toys brought into the classroom. I remember my son as a second grader took his little sister to school for show-and-tell day.

Watching a live illustration of what you are being taught is a wonderful way to learn. When you can see before your very eyes what is being said, it is so much easier to grasp. *Seeing and hearing* is one of God's major keys to instilling godly character in your life. If you want to be the kind of future leader that understands biblical principles of leadership, you must surround yourself with both *doers* and *hearers*.

If Moses, Lot, John the Baptist, the shepherds, Peter, John, Paul, and even Legion (the demoniac from Gadara) knew and understood the importance of seeing and hearing, how much more should we consider this same approach in our own lives. Think through the following examples that God has given us.

Moses' Plea

> "Hear, O Israel: The Lord our God, the Lord is one! You shall
> love the Lord your God with all your heart, with all your
> soul, and with all your strength. And these words which I
> command you today shall be in your heart. You shall teach
> them diligently to your children, and shall talk of them when
> you sit in your house, when you walk by the way, when you
> lie down, and when you rise up." *(Deuteronomy 6:4–7 NKJV)*

Moses, after receiving God's laws, cried out to every parent
who would listen to *teach* God's laws, mandates, precepts,
and principles to their children. Diligently teach them! Tell
your children what God has said. Show them how to love God
with all your heart, soul, and strength in every aspect of life.

If you have parents that show you that they love God as
they sit at home watching TV, as they go for walks with you
viewing God's creation, as they help you end your day before
bedtime with praise and thanksgiving for a wonderful day, and
as they get up early before everyone else and spend precious
time with God, show and tell others so they can listen and
learn.

What a joy when you, young lion-like leaders, leave home
knowing that you have caught what your godly parents have
taught and are not only ready to personally love God with all
your heart, soul, mind, and strength, but are ready to show
and tell your friends (and your own children someday) how
important is to love God with your entire being.

Lot's Experience

> [God] delivered righteous Lot, who was oppressed by the
> filthy conduct of the wicked (for that righteous man, dwell-
> ing among them, tormented his righteous soul from day to
> day by seeing and hearing their lawless deeds)—then the
> Lord knows how to deliver the godly out of temptations. (2
> Peter 2:7–9 NKJV)

If Lot vexed and tormented his righteous soul with "seeing
and hearing [day to day] such unlawful deeds" how much

more should we be able to encourage our souls with seeing and hearing—day after day—lion-like laws of leadership that please God.

John the Baptist's Request

Then Jesus answering said unto them, Go your way, and tell John what things ye have seen and heard; how that the blind see, the lame walk, the lepers are cleansed, the deaf hear, the dead are raised, to the poor the gospel is preached. (Luke 7:22)

John the Baptist had done his work in preparing the way for our Savior. Now, in prison, he needs some assurance that Jesus truly is the Christ, the living Son of God. Jesus sent such assurance to John by reminding John's followers to simply share what they had both *seen* and *heard*. Again, the power of seeing and hearing helped to solidify truth to John and his followers.

The Shepherds Amazement

And the shepherds returned, glorifying and praising God for all the things that they had heard and seen, as it was told unto them. (Luke 2:20)

The shepherds were changed forever. They were amazed (and afraid) as they *heard* the singing of the heavenly host announcing the birth of our Savior. But once they *saw* the Christ child in the stable area, they left glorifying and praising God for His promise of a Savior fulfilled.

Peter and John's Testimony

And they called them, and commanded them not to speak at all nor teach in the name of Jesus. But Peter and John answered and said unto them, Whether it be right in the sight of God to hearken unto you more than unto God, judge ye. For we cannot but speak the things which we have seen and heard. (Acts 4:18–20)

Peter and John were threatened with their lives to quit preaching in the name of Jesus. But knowing everything that Peter and John *heard* as they were taught by Jesus, and knowing everything that they had *seen* Jesus do as they traveled with Him for three years, they were so convinced of the truth of the gospel they couldn't help but share the wonderful story of redemption with everyone they could. Even if it meant their deaths—they didn't care. What they had seen and heard changed their lives!

Paul's Admonition

> Those things, which ye have both learned, and received, and heard, and seen in me, do: and the God of peace shall be with you. (Philippians 4:9)

God had totally changed a blasphemous, Christ-hating Saul to a loving, Christ-exalting Paul. As Paul grew and matured in the Lord, he desired the same in those he loved and encouraged. To his friends in Philippi, he simply pled with them to *do* what they have both *seen* and *heard* in his life. Paul knew the life-changing power of seeing and hearing.

The Demoniac of Gadara's Answer

Compare Luke 8:38–40 with Mark 5:18–20.

> Now the man out of whom the devils were departed besought him that he might be with him: but Jesus sent him away, saying, Return to thine own house, and **shew** how great things God hath done unto thee. And he went his way, and published throughout the whole city how great things Jesus had done unto him. (Luke 8:38–39)

> And when He got into the boat, he who had been demon-possessed begged Him that he might be with Him. However, Jesus did not permit him, but said to him, "Go home to your friends, and **tell** them what great things the Lord has done for you, and how He has had compassion on you." And he departed and began to proclaim in Decapolis all that Jesus had done for him; and all marveled. (Mark 5:18–20 NKJV)

What a wonderful transformation! The country preacher describes this guy as a "nude dude in a rude mood" who was totally changed by the power of our Lord Jesus Christ. He wanted to stay with Jesus but the Lord had other plans. Luke's account has the Lord saying, "Go home and *show* the great things that God has done for you!" and Mark says, "Go home and *tell* what great things the Lord has done for you." Although these terms are interchangeable, it does remind us that we have not only the privilege, but the obligation to *show and tell* the great things that God has done for us to every friend, family member, and acquaintance that God brings into our realm of leadership.

THE LAW OF PURPOSEFUL PURITY

─────●─────

DANIEL 1:8–9

But Daniel purposed in his heart that he would not defile himself with the portion of the king's meat, nor with the wine which he drank: therefore he requested of the prince of the eunuchs that he might not defile himself. Now God had brought Daniel into favor and tender love with the prince of the eunuchs.

Show and Tell with Your Life the Kind of Purity That Pleases God

- Show with your life that purity does not happen by accident.

- Show with your life that unless you as a young leader purposefully, doggedly, fervently, decisively, persistently, tenaciously, and eagerly pursues purity, you will not enjoy its reality in your life.

- Show with your life that purity is the unsoiled character that has successfully battled and held at bay the intense passions and unrelenting lusts of the flesh and mind.

- Show with your life that your purity is as important to you as it is to God.

- Show with your life that true purity can only be maintained from the inside out. You can't really *lose* your purity; you *give* it away.

Show and Tell That Purity of Heart Starts with the Willingness to Be Clean, Honorable, and Holy

But in a great house there are not only vessels of gold and of silver, but also of wood and of earth; and some to honor, and some to dishonor. If a man therefore purge himself from these, he shall be a vessel unto honor, sanctified, and meet for the master's use, and prepared unto every good work. Flee also youthful lusts: but follow righteousness, faith, charity, peace, with them that call on the Lord out of a pure heart. (2 Timothy 2:20–22)

What this passage is basically saying is that if any of us would dig deep into our hearts, clean house, and get rid (purge ourselves) of every filthy, stained, and impure motive, lust, fleshly desire, and inordinate passion, we could become an attractive, usable vessel of honor. We should strive to be clean, purified, sanctified, and fully prepared vessels for our wonderful Master to use any way He wants.

In a wealthy landowner's large house during the Bible times, there were many rooms completely furnished with everything needed to host honored guests in affluence and comfort. There were not only beautiful gold and silver vessels (bowls, cups, silverware, and more) used to show respect to their honored guests, but also unattractive and replaceable wood and clay vessels, normally kept out of sight in a back room. Such pots, pans, and pails were often used for waste or garbage. Their stains, cracks, and filth made them truly disgusting. No respectable host would dishonor his guests by serving them with such vessels.

Paul is telling us that we need to escape, run, and flee like fugitives from every unclean, filthy, impure, fleshly passion or lust! And as you run away from such passionate desires, keep your eye on the goal of being usable in God's hands. Do right; trust God; love both God and others; and seek peaceful relationships with everyone that God brings into your life.

Run towards righteousness. Follow after faith, charity, and peace. If you want to be consistent in this, find some friends or running mates who know how to pray and know what it means to call on the Lord out of pure hearts. You can see why it is so important for you have godly friends.

Show and Tell That Purity of Heart Impacts the Way You Handle Controversial Issues

Many young Christian college students struggle in knowing how to handle the judgmental, critical attitudes of many of their classmates. They need to be shown and taught how to go to Scripture to not only support their positions but also to shape their dispositions. This is not a new struggle. Even Paul had to encourage Timothy to keep his head on straight as he dealt with the controversial issues that caused disagreement among good men.

> As I besought thee to abide still at Ephesus, when I went into Macedonia, that thou mightest charge some that they teach no other doctrine, neither give heed to fables and endless genealogies, which minister questions, rather than godly edifying which is in faith: so do. Now the end of the commandment is charity [love] out of a **pure heart**, and of a good conscience, and of faith unfeigned. From which some having swerved have turned aside unto vain jangling; desiring to be teachers of the law; understanding neither what they say, nor whereof they affirm. (1 Timothy 1:3–7)

Paul left Timothy in charge to charge the squabbling Ephesian believers to stop focusing on controversial issues rather than the work of God.

Some in Timothy's day were devoted to, focused on, and consumed with issues that were distracting them from edifying believers and magnifying the gospel. Basically God told

Paul to tell Timothy to tell others to replace their meaningless discussions with a meaningful love that comes from a pure heart, a clear conscience, and a sincere, genuine faith. The purpose of God's instruction was that all believers would be filled with such love.

A First Timothy, Chapter One person loves out of a pure heart which involves a motivational love that is clean, pure, and clear. This kind of person's heart is unsoiled and unalloyed. An unsoiled heart has kept itself unstained from the heart sins of greed, pride, envy, lust, strife, contention, and bitterness. An unalloyed heart of love is not mixed with selfish agendas or personal interests. It simply and genuinely loves others and seeks their good even if it means unexpected sacrifice or a limitation of its liberties.

A First Timothy, Chapter One person loves out of a good, clear conscience which in the sight of God is of great value. A clear conscience presupposes that all sins and offenses have been confessed and forsaken. A clear conscience is not a secret keeper. It gives God—and anyone else who desires to know—the password into its inner thoughts, because it has nothing to hide. A First Timothy 1:5 person is free to love without fear of the past coming to light, revealing some cover-up or some ulterior motive for such love.

A First Timothy, Chapter One person also loves out of a real, sincere, genuine faith. Unfeigned faith has stepped off the stage and refuses to pretend that it is something that it is not. There is no hypocrisy, no pretense, just real, genuine, sincere faith. It never takes on the role of a giant pretending to be bigger than it really is, but it is willing to be compared to a tiny, little mustard seed. It knows it can grow, and therefore purposely engulfs itself in the Word of God, which is the key to its growth and maturity. It never allows external righteousness to make others think that it is bigger and stronger than it really is. It admits its weakness and cries out to God to increase and strengthen it. Unfeigned faith refuses to wear a mask. It does not pretend to be a sin hater in public while at the same time loving sin in private. It is real.

Show and Tell That the Desire for Purity Is Both Courageous and Contagious.

Let no man despise thy youth; but **be thou an example** of the believers, in word, in conversation, in charity, in spirit, in faith, **in purity**. (1 Timothy 4:12)

Many of you wrestle with how to make 1 Timothy 4:12 a reality in your everyday lives. You are not sure how to keep your parents, leaders, and even younger friends or siblings from despising your youthfulness or looking down on you just because you are young.

Strong spiritual leaders are not defined by age. It takes a bit of courage—lion-like courage—to make a difference today. Don't let anyone look down on you just because you are young! Don't let them ever accuse you of youthful inconsistencies in your lifestyle or attitude. Be careful to not fall prey to youthful idleness. Study God's Word; be generous to those who are hurting; increase your stability in what you believe. Don't let anyone look down on you because of youthful indiscretion or impulsiveness in areas of purity of mind, purity of body, and purity of conscience. If you really want to be a lion-like leader someday, be an example now to both those older than you—that's parents and leaders—and those younger than you—even your precious little brothers and sisters. Show all of us how to be pure and stay pure. If you stay busy being an example in word, lifestyle, love, spirit, and faith you won't have time to do anything else! You see, your courageous leadership to all of us can be quite contagious. Your brothers and sisters will want to follow your example. Hopefully you see why your example is so important. Just try to be the example to others that your Lord has been to you.

Show with your life that the desire for purity in all areas is both courageous and contagious.

Show and Tell That a Pure Heart Leads to a Blessed Life

Blessed are the pure in heart: for they shall see God. (Matthew 5:8)

Whether you say it as one syllable—*blessed*—or two—*bles-sed*—it is a wonderful word, a wonderful principle, and a wonderful feeling. To be blessed. To feel blessed. To know that someone loves you enough to bless you. True biblical blessing from God is much more than the "bless your heart" from a southern-fried greeting. *Blessed* differs from the word *happy* in that the root *hap* has the idea of luck, fortune, or chance. The *blessed* (*makarios*) is the one who is in the world yet independent of the world, and his satisfaction comes from God and not from favorable circumstances.

Such blessedness is reserved for those who are pure in heart. David, Paul, and Peter all agree that such purity of heart is seen in sincere individuals—men who think, speak, and act without hypocrisy. Sometime get your Bible out and study Psalm 73:1; 1 Timothy 1:5; 2 Timothy 2:22; and 1 Peter 1:22.

The New Testament Commentary by Hendriksen and Kistemaker states this:

> The greatest blessing to those who are pure in heart is the promise of seeing God! Now, here on earth we still see *in a mirror darkly* but in heaven and in the renewed universe, our vision will amount to the sinless and uninterrupted fellowship of the souls of all the redeemed with God in Christ, a seeing "face to face" (1 Corinthians 13:12).[1]

This will be an answer to the prayer of Jesus in John 17:24, "Father, I desire that they also whom You gave Me may be with Me where I am, that they may behold [gaze on] My glory which You have given Me, for You loved Me before the foundation of the world" (NKJV).

As sweet and *blessed* as this truth is, a view of the same verse in a rearview mirror is a warning that we all must heed. "Cursed forever are the impure in heart whose insincerity, hypocrisy, and pretense will make it possible that they will only see God on their judgment day—but never again."

Let one of your young friends know today that a pure heart leads to a blessed life.

Show and Tell That Purity Knows What a Good Friend Looks Like

Finally, brethren, whatsoever things are true, whatsoever things are honest, whatsoever things are just, whatsoever things are pure, whatsoever things are lovely, whatsoever things are of good report; if there be any virtue, and if there be any praise, think on these things. (Philippians 4:8)

You can tell a lot about a person by the friends he or she hangs out with. **Purity** has some wonderful friends. Let me introduce them to you.

- First, there is **Truth**. He is an unchanging, stable friend.

- Over there is **Honest** (we call him Noble), and you will never find a more excellent and dignified friend than he.

- Next to him is **Just**, and he is one of the most fair and balanced guys you will ever know. You are confident that he will always choose to do right.

- Then there is **Lovely**, and she is just what her name says—a dear, loving friend who is always there for you. You will never hear her say anything off-color or mean.

- Over there in the corner is **Good Report**. I've never heard anyone gossip or have anything bad to say about him.

- **Virtue** is one of those friends that everyone would love to have as a best friend. She is a sweet, pure, morally excellent girl and a perfect example for all girls to follow.

- Finally I see **Praise**. He is *thanksgiving* in body. You cannot hang with him very long before you are praising and thanking God for His goodness and grace.

Seven good friends. Think about them! Just thinking about each one and their potential influence can encourage your heart. Purity's friends are the kinds of friends all of us need to find.

Show and Tell That Purity of Conscience Is a Qualification for Godly, Spiritual Leaders

Holding the mystery of the faith in [with] a **pure conscience**. (1 Timothy 3:9)

Learn to look for real life situations that teach eternal truths. For instance, suppose your family is tobogganing down a steep hill and halfway down your junior high brother lets go of the toboggan and face plants in the snow at the bottom of the hill. Once inside, with a cup of hot chocolate in hand, the dialog could possibly go something like this.

Dad: Nice ride. Actually, it was quite funny (once I knew you weren't hurt). You know, your ride down the hill reminds me of the verses we read this morning in our family devotions. Do you remember that one short verse that talked about a pure conscience?

Son: Yeah! Something like, "holding on to your faith with a pure conscience?"

Dad: Close. "Holding the mystery of the faith with a pure conscience." The *holding* is what you forgot to do on your speed ride down the hill.

If you guys want to be true, spiritual leaders, you will need to learn to hold on, cling to, or hold fast to the mystery of the faith. You will not always understand every aspect of your faith, but you must believe with a pure conscience. You cannot be distracted nor have your grip weakened with character or actions that are undignified, double-tongued, controlled by any addictive substances, or greedy! Such actions and attitudes will create an impure conscience which results in weakness of character. Such lack of character then lets go of its faith in Christ while it holds on to its impurity. Only those with a truly pure conscience can get a grip that holds so tightly it won't let go no matter who or what seeks to pull it away.

Son: Thanks dad. Keep praying for me that I'll tightly hold on to my relationship with God better than I did the toboggan.

Show and Tell That Your Daily Worship Is Impacted by Purity

Pure religion and undefiled before God and the Father is this, to visit the fatherless and widows in their affliction [trouble, distress], and to keep himself unspotted [unstained, unpolluted, unblemished, uncorrupted] from the world. (James 1:27)

James has a way of simplifying serious truths so that all of us can understand what he is saying. In our world where *worship* is discussed and defined in a variety of ways, we can go back to the roots of *threskeia*, which means "worship of God referred to as religion" and see that God's view of genuine, undefiled, untouched by music, moods, or mics kind of worship is two fold.

First of all, pure religion involves caring for those who are in distress and cannot pay you back in any way—like orphans and widows. This checks your heart's motivation. Such a mindset has nothing to do with prestige, popularity, fundraising, politics, or pride. Saying yes to others in need with a genuine willingness to sacrifice for them is pure religion in God's eyes.

Secondly, pure religion also involves keeping yourself pure from the world's corrupting, polluting, and defiling influences. This is a great way to not only examine your loyalty to the Lord but to also reveal your spiritual maturity. As you apply biblical principles to life's ethical, moral, and influential choices, you will refuse to insist on your own rights. Learn to say no to self in order to minister to others. We read in 1 Peter 1:19 that our Lord was without spot. 1 Timothy 6:14 teaches us that our doctrine is to be without spot.

If you asked David about this, he would say, "Let me teach you how to walk" and then would probably quote Psalm 119:1–3.

> Blessed are the undefiled in the way, who walk in the law of the Lord. Blessed are they that keep His testimonies, and that seek Him with the whole heart. They also do no iniquity: they walk in His ways.

If you questioned Isaiah, he would say, "Wash up and help me serve" and then share Isaiah 1:16–18 with you.

> Wash you, make you clean; put away the evil of your doings from before mine eyes; cease to do evil; learn to do well; seek judgment, relieve the oppressed, judge the fatherless, plead for the widow. Come now, and let us reason together, saith the Lord: though your sins be as scarlet, they shall be as white as snow; though they be red like crimson, they shall be as wool.

John would lay it on the line with a put-up-or-shut-up philosophy of living and giving as he wrote in 1 John 3:17–18.

But whoso hath this world's good, and seeth his brother have need, and shutteth up his bowels of compassion from him, how dwelleth the love of God in him? My little children, let us not love in word, neither in tongue; but in deed and in truth.

Your daily worship is impacted by purity.

Show and Tell That You Can't Argue with Pure Wisdom

JAMES 3:17–18

But the wisdom that is from above is first pure, then peaceable, gentle, and easy to be entreated [open to reason, willing to yield], full of mercy and good fruits, without partiality [unwavering], and without hypocrisy. And the fruit of righteousness is sown in peace of them that make peace.

Would you consider yourself an argumentative person? Do you have professional quarrelers in your home? When we are prone to argue and quarrel, we usually think that we are right, and we want to get our opinions across. There is a great lesson in James 3 that shows us that sometimes we might be right, but are actually wrong in the way we try to prove we are right.

James 3:17–18 is all about pure wisdom. What do you really see when you gaze into pure, peaceful, gentle, approachable, merciful, fruitful, impartial, unhypocritical wisdom? Well, James is certainly painting a picture with some definite and vivid contrasts here by his use of the conjunction *but*. Wisdom that comes from God is pure, clean, and free from the defilements and impurities listed in the four preceding verses.

Who is a wise man and endued with knowledge among you? Let him shew out of a good conversation his works with meekness of wisdom. But if ye have bitter envying and strife in your hearts, glory not, and lie not against the truth. This wisdom descendeth not from above, but is earthly, sensual, devilish. For where envying and strife is, there is confusion and every evil work. (James 3:13–16)

Godly, heavenly, reasonable, and peaceable wisdom refuses to be spotted, stained, or polluted by bitter jealousy or selfish ambition. Godly wisdom never says, "my way or the highway." Godly wisdom is open to reason, serious study, and is always willing to yield where it has misapplied Scriptural principles. Although pure wisdom has an open mind, it is not so open that its brains have fallen out. It does not give in to partiality but is unwavering in areas of undeniable truth. Pure wisdom is not wishy-washy, easily swayed, or wind driven, but firmly takes a gentle stand with a peaceful, peace-loving and peace-making attitude of heart.

Show and Tell That True Love Comes from a Pure Heart

Seeing ye have purified your souls in obeying the truth through the Spirit unto unfeigned [sincere, unpretentious] love of the brethren, see that ye love one another with a pure heart fervently. (1 Peter 1:22)

As you know, teenagers tend to be critical. You can spend way too much time cutting each other down. Sad to say, you often mirror what you see in the adults around you. Too often you pretend to love rather than practicing true, biblical love.

How do you love deeply from the heart? What does fervent love from a pure heart look like? A deep love that comes straight from the heart erases strife, abolishes hypocrisy, eliminates tension, and totally annihilates jealousy. Purify yourselves by obeying the truth, and you will have a sincere, deep love for your brothers. In other words, take the divinely enabled love that God put into your selfish heart and use it! God already changed your heart to help you stop loving self and start loving others, so keep that change going, don't quit loving, but change the recipient of your love from yourself to others.

Show and Tell That the First Step to Purity Is a Step Towards Christlikeness

One simple principle that will help all of us stay pure in our thoughts, in our motives, and in our lives is found hidden in 1 John 3:1–3.

> Behold, what manner [kind] of love the Father hath bestowed upon [given] us, that we should be called the sons [children] of God: therefore the world knoweth us not, because it knew him not. Beloved, now are we the sons of God, and it doth not yet appear what we shall be: but we know that, when he shall appear, we shall be like him; for we shall see him as he is. And every man that has this hope in him purifieth himself, even as he is pure.

What kind of love comes from God? Since God is pure and holy, we know that God's love has to be a pure kind of love which is free from the silliness, the selfishness, and the sinfulness of man. It is the kind of love that loves the unlovely; the kind of love that is kind to the unkind; the kind of love that is faithful to the unfaithful. You cannot really describe it without going to the cross. You cannot really define it in human terms. You can accept it and be thankful for it without even totally understanding it. There is much more that we *do not know* than what we *do know* about our eternal state. In many ways we will be like our risen Lord, but not in all ways. God's incommunicable, God-only *omni* traits such as His omniscience, His omnipotence, and His omnipresence are characteristics that we will praise Him for throughout eternity.

John states a fact here—not a wish, not a possibility, not a command, just a fact. The fact is that every man that has the hope of becoming more and more like Jesus Christ and being conformed to His image will purify himself. The standard is set. When I was a little kid, I could not draw at all. Then I got the great idea that if I took my black crayon and placed a sheet of white paper over my coloring book, I could trace the picture, and it would look like I could draw. The closer I stayed to the pattern, the better tracing I got.

The closer we stay to Christ, the better tracing we will get.

Commentators Kistemaker and Hendriksen state it this way.

> The believer lives in the hope of becoming conformed to Jesus Christ, and the more he contemplates this truth the more he purifies himself of sin. He seeks to cleanse himself from sin that contaminates body and soul; constantly he strives for holiness in reverence to God. (2 Cor. 7:1)[2]

So, simply said, if you want to stay pure, take a step towards Christlikeness. The more you are like Christ, the more pure you will be. The more you are like Christ the more excited you will be to see Him face to face.

THE LAW OF TRUSTWORTHINESS
———————•———————

DANIEL 6:1–2

It pleased Darius to set over the kingdom an hundred and twenty princes, which should be over the whole kingdom; and over these three presidents; of whom Daniel was first: that the princes might give accounts unto them, and the king should have no damage.

Show and Tell with Your Life the Kind of Trustworthiness That Pleases God

Daniel was a trustworthy man, but his trustworthiness did not start when he reached his eightieth birthday. Even as a young teen, he earned a respectable position that came from being trustworthy.

Trust can be earned. Trust can be lost. Trust can be gained. Trust can be wasted. As much as a high yield bearing financial IRA (Individual Retirement Account) is essential for a comfortable retirement, a spiritual ITA (Individual Trust Account) is essential for godly relationships and influence. What we put into our trust accounts will determine the extent of our influence as leaders. Although it takes years to build up a strong trust account, we can bankrupt our accounts with one foolish, selfish, sinful decision. In regards to trust, we can go from millionaire status to poverty level by one wrong choice. It takes only a short amount of time to clear up a

Chapter 11 Bankruptcy status; it takes a lifetime to eliminate mistrust.

Trust takes years to build and seconds to shatter.

So, anyone who wants to be a spiritual leader—especially a leader with lion-like character—has to be willing to face some hard questions.

- Are you trustworthy?

- Can others trust you to be on time for work, for church, or for anything?

- Teen guys, can a dad trust you with his daughter? Teen girls, can a dad trust you with his son?

- Can you be trusted to do a job quickly and completely?

- Can you be trusted to be attentive to details with a spirit of excellence?

- Are you reliable? Are you dependable? Are you responsible? Are you trustworthy?

- Do others believe in you or doubt your sincerity?

- Can you be trusted with the TV remote or unfiltered Internet?

- Can you be trusted with confidential information?

- Can you be trusted to do what you promise to do?

Take a minute and read the following statements carefully and prayerfully. Then ask yourself if these principles should in any way change the way you think or act.

- Trust is a solid foundation for all solid friendships.

- When leaders fulfill what they consent to do, even if it means unexpected sacrifice; when they make their own schedules and priorities secondary to the wishes of those they are serving; when they are determined to accomplish God's goals regardless of the opposition; and when they continue steadfastly despite the difficulties, they can be trusted by both God and those whom they are serving.

- "If you find an honest, dependable, reliable, and responsible teen, hire him." (source unknown)

- If you are trusted, you'll never be alone. If you are trusted, you'll never be without ministry. If you are trusted, you'll have opportunities to serve God unknown to the untrustworthy.

- Trust is like a mirror: once it is broken, you can never look at it quite right again.

- Behind every untrusting girl or guy is someone who taught them to be that way.

- "What upsets me is not that you lied to me, but that from now on I can no longer believe you." (source unknown, but thought by many)

Show and Tell That Trustworthiness Is Best Friends with Faithfulness

A talebearer revealeth secrets: but he that is of a faithful spirit concealeth the matter. (Proverbs 11:13)

Whoever goes about slandering reveals secrets, but he who is trustworthy in spirit keeps a thing covered. (Proverbs 11:13 ESV)

Have you ever wondered who can you trust? Have you ever shared a very personal secret with a close friend and within the hour everyone in the cyberworld knew about it? Talebearers will die very lonely people.

Anyone who has a faithful spirit is trustworthy. You can trust them with all your heart. You can share anything and everything, knowing that you will get the counsel, help, and encouragement you seek without being exposed on that person's Facebook wall the next day. The trustworthy person does not gain friends or seek acceptance by spreading gossip, which, by the way, has a negative slant just by its very nature.

Very few gossip about a guy who just led his friend to the Lord. Very few gossip about a pastor's early hours in prayer for his people. Very few gossip about a boy's heavy involvement in Scripture memory to keep his heart and mind pure. Gossips only like to share the "bad stuff" to cause others to think little of others and more of them. Gossips are far from trustworthy.

Show and Tell That Trustworthiness Is Big When It Comes to Little Things

He that is faithful [trustworthy] in that which is least [the little things, a very small matter] is faithful [trustworthy] also in much [the big things, important matters]: and he that is unjust [untrustworthy] in the least [the little things, a very small matter] is unjust [untrustworthy] also in much [the big things, important matters]. If therefore ye have not been faithful in the unrighteous mammon [wealth], who will **commit to your trust** [entrust, count you as trustworthy] the true riches? And if ye have not been faithful in that which is another man's [someone else's property—namely God], who shall give you that which is your own? No servant can serve two masters: for either he will hate the one, and love the other; or else he will hold to [be devoted to] the one, and despise the other. Ye cannot serve God and mammon [wealth]. (Luke 16:10–13)

Little things in life can become big things in eternity.

Our trustworthiness is easily tested and tried with something small—a small task, a small investment, a small responsibility, or a small leadership opportunity. Those doing the testing are careful not to risk too much loss should those entrusted become untrustworthy.

A pastor will think, "Let me see how you prepare and plan for your fourth grade Sunday school class before you begin working with the College and Career group."

A restaurant employer will think, "Let me see if he can be on time for two weeks in a row before I promote him to manager."

A new boss will think, "Let's test this guy's contentment and see how hard he works for minimum wage before I start increasing his pay scale."

A dad thinks, "I'll watch and see how he takes care of our family car—keeps it clean, gasses it up—before I shock him with a car of his own."

A college girl thinks, "I want to see how he treats me with respect and challenges me spiritually before I commit to anything serious in this relationship."

Until we recognize that God has given us—actually, entrusted us with—everything we have, and until our possessions are defined by the words *His* and not *my*, we will be lacking in our trust account with God. Nabal, the Old Testament fool in 1 Samuel 25:11 (ESV) talked about "*my* bread and *my* water and *my* meat . . . for *my* shearers." The rich fool found in Luke 12:16–21 in the New Testament talked about "*my* barns . . . *my* fruits and *my* goods." Both foolishly went out into eternity with a zero balance in their trust accounts.

Although there are many areas of life that are impacted by trustworthiness, three that seem to stand out are time, talents, and treasures.

If we can be depended on to be on time, even early, we will gain great confidence from our leaders. Each time we are five or ten minutes late, a small withdrawal is made from our accounts.

God gives giftedness (talents) and waits to see if those divinely enabled gifts are buried, hidden, used for self-exaltation, or used to draw men's attention to Him. Hide it under a bushel? No! Blessing three elderly ladies at a nursing home with a song of comfort is as important to God as filling a concert hall.

When it comes to treasures, even as teens, the more we have, the more we think we deserve what we have and probably a little more. What goes first in times of financial pressure? Entertainment? Eating out? Internet access? Tithe or offering?

When we view our little time, tiny talents, and trivial treasures as gifts from God and use them for God and others, our trust accounts will skyrocket higher than S&P or Wall Street could even imagine. Stay faithful in the little things, and when Christ returns we will realize a great return.

Show and Tell That Trustworthiness Is Fulfilling the Cause You Were Born for

A friend loveth at all times, and a brother is born for adversity. (Proverbs 17:17)

You've probably heard this exchange of words. "Are you ready?" "Ready! I was born ready." What were you born for? Why are you here on earth right now? Those who have attached themselves to a cause bigger than themselves often see their entire existence wrapped around that cause. Obviously, the cause of Christ is a wonderful cause to be identified with, to live for, to be motivated by, and to be born to. Jesus came not to be served or ministered to, but to serve others. Others-focused! His cause was wrapped up in the ministry of reconciliation as He gave His life to "bring us to God." We are born to love others to the Lord. When we realize that we are here on earth to serve others and glorify God, we have a purpose for living and a cause to get us out of bed each morning.

True friends have an *I'm there!* mindset. You need help? I'm there. Are you going through a tough time? I'm there. When the grief is great and the suffering is almost unbearable, I will be by your side. This is why I am here. This is what I was born for. True friends and loving brothers are born to live for others. Our Lord Jesus Christ was born to die. What were you born for?

Show and Tell That Trustworthiness Always Keeps His Word

If a man vow a vow unto the Lord, or swear an oath to bind his soul with a bond; he shall not break his word, he shall do according to all that proceedeth out of his mouth. (Numbers 30:2)

A trustworthy leader says what he will do and does what he has said. You can **trust** what he says! Unlike pragmatic politicians or money-hungry businessmen of today, there was a day when a man's word was his honor. He would never go back on his promise but would do what he said he would do. No contracts. No notarized signatures. A man's word was enough. If he said he would be there, he would be. If he said he would pay for it, it would be paid for. If he said he would fix it free of charge, it would be done. Trustworthy men are not easily swayed, easily sidetracked, easily discouraged, or easily manipulated. What he says, what he promises, he will do. We have a perfect example in our Lord. What He promises He fulfills.

- God promised to send a Redeemer. He did.

- God promised our Savior would be born in Bethlehem. He was.

- God promised to send His Holy Spirit. He came.

- God promised to come back to earth someday. He will.

THE LAW OF EXCELLENCE
———————•———————

DANIEL 6:3

Then this Daniel was preferred above the presidents and princes, because an **excellent spirit** was in him; and the king thought to set him over the whole realm.

Show and Tell with Your Life the Kind of Excellence That Pleases God

What did Daniel have that most in our world lack? Daniel had an excellent spirit about him.

It is sad that we live in a day when the idolatrous and the idle are elevated to the level of the industrious and intelligent. The silent war on excellence attempts to keep everyone equal so that no one feels inferior. It is almost intolerable today to be excellent in your morals, excellent in your integrity, or excellent in your relationship with God. Don't let feelings of inferiority get you down. Instead, use them to motivate you to follow the example of those who are superior in godliness and righteousness.

Leaders need to know what words or attitudes could diminish the outstanding quality of their work or what actions could distract someone's attention away from excellence.

Leaders need to work hard to keep mediocrity from becoming the accepted norm.

We must not spend our lives attacking mediocrity, but instead, enjoy the pursuit of excellence.

Living on the extreme, radical edge of what is great keeps us from being satisfied with the good-OK-fair-stay-above-C-level kind of living.

God is a God of excellence in character, in power, and in wisdom. All that He is and all that He does is excellent, superb, and incredibly superior to all others.

God's excellence in character enables me to worship Him with awe and reverential fear. If I could attain such superiority, I would not be overwhelmed with such greatness.

Show and Tell That As We Serve an Excellent God, We Must Do So with an Excellent Spirit

Then this Daniel was preferred above the presidents and princes, because an **excellent spirit** was in him; and the king thought to set him over the whole realm. (Daniel 6:3)

Why did King Darius prefer Daniel over the others? What caused Daniel to distinguish himself above the other leaders? It was not his youthful enthusiasm; at this time he was over eighty! It was not his popularity. Daniel was ganged up on—122 against 1—but even with such odds, King Darius preferred the 1 over the 122. It was nothing external— appearance, wealth, political ties, celebrity status. Darius was impressed with Daniel's "excellent spirit."

An Excellent Spirit Was in Him . . .

Daniel had a spirit, an attitude, a way about him, that as he did his work and mingled with his coworkers, he surpassed the spirits and attitudes of all those around him. He was not moody. He could not be accused of being lazy. He obviously was not spacey or forgetful. He was different than those around him. All were leaders with influence and intelligence.

But Daniel possessed something that the others lacked. Here is a true picture of *divinely enabled leadership,* for such a superior, excellent spirit comes only from God. Although Daniel was not a superhero, he did possess a supernatural power. He was supernaturally controlled by God's amazing (excellent) grace! God gives grace to only the humble—those who put Him and others before themselves, as did Daniel for his eighty plus years. The 122 were proud, envious men in which God's grace refuses to abide. Daniel was a grace filled leader known for his excellent spirit.

Show and Tell That God Is Excellent in His Greatness

Wherefore thou art great, O Lord God: for there is none like thee, neither is there any God beside thee, according to all that we have heard with our ears. (2 Samuel 7:22)

Little kids are often taught to pray, "God is great. God is good. Let us thank Him for our food. Amen." But they are never taught how God's excellence should impact their lives.

The words *excellence* and *greatness* are almost synonymous. God is not average; He is great! God is not mediocre, He is great! God is not just OK; He is great! In our world, *good* means *just OK.* It is not great; neither is it bad. It is just enough to get by. In a way, *good* could be an enemy of *great.*

To say that God is excellent means that He excels in His greatness. He is not satisfied with just being good in His love; He is great in His love and there is none who love as deeply and as passionately as God. God is not content to be OK in His kindness; He is great in His kindness, and there is no one who cares as much as God. God never stops at just *good* but always goes right on to *great.*

God's greatness is seen in His life on earth. Jesus Christ is the visible icon of the invisible God. Jesus was not satisfied to be just a good teenager; He sought excellence as He increased in wisdom, stature, and in favor with God and with man. Jesus was excellent in His love which He displayed when He voluntarily gave up His life on the cross. Jesus was excellent in His power when He defeated death and rose from the grave. Jesus left us an example of greatness.

Show and Tell That God's Excellence Is Incomparable to Anyone or Anything

For who in the heaven can be compared unto the Lord? who among the sons of the mighty can be likened unto the Lord? God is greatly to be feared in the assembly of the saints, and to be had in reverence of all them that are about Him. (Psalm 89:6–7)

It is never wise to compare yourself with others, but it is a humbling thing to compare yourself with God. It is not only humbling but a great way to live in reality. David may have struggled with the same issue when he wrote Psalm 89:6–7.

Comparing yourself with others could result in pride and arrogance, especially when you compare with those less fortunate, less talented, or less attractive. Comparing yourself with God reveals the selfish, sinful soul you really are. God sets a standard of excellence that we must strive for but will never attain until we are released and rescued from these sin-cursed bodies. Knowing my own deficiencies only makes me more overwhelmed and amazed at God's excellencies. Heaven will be filled with wonderful people and magnificent angels, but none will even begin to compare with our excellent Lord God. Mighty men have walked the earth—mighty in strength, mighty in brilliance, mighty in influence, and mighty in appearance—but even the mightiest man that ever walked on earth pales in comparison to the Lord God. Those who have taken the time to really get to know God in all His excellencies will hold Him with utmost respect and a reverential awe. There are a number of hymns that express God's unique excellence that you can meditate on.

Show and Tell That God's Excellence Is Like No Others

The more you realize how wonderful and excellent God is, the more you want to praise Him. In fact at eighty years of age Daniel still prayed to God three times a day.

Eighty year old Moses sang a song of praise to God. I would have loved to hear that old guy sing. The lyrics of his song are in Exodus 15:11.

> "Who is like You, O Lord, among the gods? Who is like You, glorious in holiness, fearful in praises, doing wonders?" (NKJV)

Moses saw God's power and protection in such overwhelming glory it still thrills our hearts when we read what God did that day. Imagine standing with your own family, huddled together on the sandy coastline of the Red Sea as the enormous Egyptian army raced toward you in their chariots with their bloodthirsty spears lifted ready to kill those you love so much. Imagine the fear. Imagine seeing what God did. It would make you want to step up alongside of Moses and turn his solo into a duet: "Who is like You, O Lord among the gods? Who is like You, glorious in holiness, fearful in praises, doing wonders?"

What happened that prompted Moses to sing this song?

> Now it came to pass, in the morning watch, that the Lord looked down upon the army of the Egyptians through the pillar of fire and cloud, and He troubled the army of the Egyptians. And He took off their chariot wheels, so that

they drove them with difficulty; and the Egyptians said, "Let us flee from the face of Israel, for the Lord fights for them against the Egyptians."

Then the Lord said to Moses, "Stretch out your hand over the sea that the waters may come back upon the Egyptians, on their chariots, and on their horsemen." And Moses stretched out his hand over the sea; and when the morning appeared, the sea returned to its full depth, while the Egyptians were fleeing into it. So the Lord overthrew the Egyptians in the midst of the sea. Then the waters returned and covered the chariots, the horsemen, and all the army of Pharaoh that came into the sea after them. Not so much as one of them remained. But the children of Israel had walked on dry land in the midst of the sea, and the waters were a wall to them on their right hand and on their left.

So the Lord saved Israel that day out of the hand of the Egyptians, and Israel saw the Egyptians dead on the seashore. Thus Israel saw the great work which the Lord had done in Egypt; so the people feared the Lord, and believed the Lord and His servant Moses. (Exodus 14:24–31 NKJV)

Meditate on this, and you will be able to sing when you are eighty!

Show and Tell That Love Is the More Excellent Way

Never underestimate the importance of love. Excellent love. Have you ever had part in a conversation like the one below?

Sara: Dad, do you think I'll ever win anything? It seems that every time I enter any competition, there is always someone much better than me. I'm not saying that they *aren't* better, because they are. And I want them to excel and even get better. But what do I have to offer? I can play the piano, but not like Irene. I can sing, but not like Christina. I am not bad at art, but I'm not good like Scott. You know my volleyball skills—no Olympic team for me. It's really not a lot of fun to be an ordinary, average, boring person.

Dad: Sara, you are forgetting your best gift. I really don't know of another sixteen-year-old girl as kind and loving as you. At church the little kids love you, and the senior saints adore you. If you remember the pastor's series on 1 Corinthians 13, you remember that even the most gifted of all people pale in comparison to those who love. I scribbled some thoughts from the pastor's messages and kind of rewrote part of the passage from the opposite view. You read Paul's account, and then I'll read the same thing from kind of a mirrored view. Then we will see which one you would rather be known for.

Sara: OK. I'll start with the last verse of chapter 12. "But earnestly desire the best gifts. And yet I show you a more excellent way. Though I speak with the tongues of men and of angels, but have not love, I have become sounding brass or a clanging cymbal. And though I have the gift of prophecy, and understand all mysteries and all knowledge, and though I have all faith, so that I could remove mountains, but have not love, I am nothing. And though I bestow all my goods to feed the poor, and though I give my body to be burned, but have not love, it profits me nothing. Love suffers long and is kind; love does not envy; love does not parade itself, is not puffed up; does not behave rudely, does not seek its own, is not provoked, thinks no evil; does not rejoice in iniquity, but rejoices in the truth; bears all things, believes all things, hopes all things, endures all things." Your turn.

Dad: Ok, now looking at the same passage from an opposing view. 'Unloving people will be known for their impatience, even their harsh unkindness at times. They will be jealous and envious of others. Their pride will be evident in the way they boast and constantly talk about themselves. They can be rude and self-seeking at times. Unloving people are usually angry people who easily and often lose their tempers. Some bitterly hold grudges against others and actually think that sin is fun. They look out for themselves and no one else, are doubtful and suspicious, they often are quite negative and have a hard time seeing the good in any situation or any person. You can't count on them. When things get hard, they easily give up and quit." They have life all backwards. They live a mirrored view of 1 Corinthians 13.

Sara: Got it dad. Thanks for always taking me to the Bible.

Never underestimate the importance of excellent love. If we look, we will be amazed at the many opportunities God allows in our lives to communicate the excellence of true biblical love. Lion-like leaders are loving leaders. Excellence in leadership is wrapped in excellent, unselfish love.

Show and Tell That As Your Love Grows, Your Understanding of Excellence Will Increase

And this I pray, that your love may abound yet more and more in knowledge and in all judgment; that ye may approve things that are excellent; that ye may be sincere and without offence till the day of Christ. (Philippians 1:9–10)

Even though you know that your parents and leaders want the best for you, it is hard to understand why you are being told no so often. If you could just understand the reasoning behind their thinking, it would help you to accept the restrictions and lessen the stress that often comes with the necessary negatives in life.

Some areas of life are more controversial and therefore more stressful than others. No leader will hit a home run every time. The most controversial and emotional questions seem to involve various types of electronic entertainment. Let's group movies, music, TV, Internet, and all social media under that label. Read Philippians 1:9–10 again.

> And this I pray, that your love may abound yet more and more in knowledge and in all judgment; that ye may approve things that are excellent; that ye may be sincere and without offence till the day of Christ.

Here is what *The New Testament Commentary* by William Hendriksen and Simon J. Kistemaker says about this passage.

> Certain commentators here prefer the rendering "so that you may distinguish the things that differ." In the abstract this translation is possible. Besides, the difference between the two is not great, for the ability to distinguish between the good and the bad would be for the purpose of electing the former and rejecting the latter . . . the man who not only has the ability to distinguish but also actually chooses the things that really matter, in preference to those that are either bad or of little importance, does this with a view to being "pure and blameless." Underlying the first adjective (pure) is probably the image of precious metal from which the dross has been removed; hence, unmixed, without alloy; and so, in the moral sense, pure. Underlying the second (blameless) is that of arriving at one's destination not stumbled against, i.e., uninjured by any obstacles in the road; hence, morally uninjured, and so, not worthy of blame, blameless. The prayer, then, is that the Philippians, their faculties having been trained to prefer the good to the evil, and the essential to the trivial, may be pure and blameless with a view to the day of Christ. For the expression "the day of Christ" . . . Their whole life must be

a preparation for that great day, for it is then that the true character of every man's life will be revealed (1 Cor. 3:10-15), and everyone will be judged according to his work (Dan. 7:10; Mal. 3:16; Matt. 25:31–46; Luke 12:3; 1 Cor. 4:5; Rev. 20:12).[1]

As a lion-like leader, your decisions should be motivated by love—love for God and love for others. Nurturing the desire to stay morally pure, and as the commentator's said it, morally uninjured or unscarred, is not always easy, but definitely necessary.

The phrase "so that you may approve things that are excellent" means that you not only know what is best, but you choose the best.

The kind of unselfish love God puts into your hearts will be evident in the following ways.

- Your love will overflow and keep overflowing. It is not a mood or a temporary act of kindness but a love that lasts.

- You will be more understanding and discerning in what you say and do.

- You will weigh others' words and actions in a way that you will be able to discern not just between the good and the bad, but also the good and the excellent.

- You will be real, sincere—not phony or fake in any way.

- Your life will accomplish great things for God and impact others.

- It will be evident that God is very pleased with the way you are living.

In other words,

- *your love will abound yet more and more in knowledge and in all judgment;*

- *you will approve things that are excellent;*

- *you will be sincere and without offence till the day of Christ; and*

- *you will be filled with the fruits of righteousness, which are by Jesus Christ, unto the glory and praise of God.*

THE LAW OF FAITHFULNESS

DANIEL 6:4

Then the presidents and princes sought to find occasion against Daniel concerning the kingdom; but they could find none occasion nor fault; forasmuch as he was **faithful**.

Show and Tell with Your Life the Kind of Faithfulness That Pleases God

A faithful leader is not only trustworthy, but loyal to those God has called him to serve; he never allows weariness, adversity, or hardships to deter him from his commitment. Faithfulness is dependability with its shoes on. Faithfulness is doing what you promised to do! No questions. No excuses. No complaints.

God is the perfect judge of faithfulness. He is the only one that knows if we are as faithful in our private lives as we are in our public lives.

Faithful, lion-like leaders are totally dependent on three things:

1. God's living and powerful Word to renew their minds.

2. God's enabling grace to give both the power and the desire for such faithfulness.

3. God's empowering Spirit to help them refuse the downward pull of their unfaithful flesh.

Faithfulness is on God's list of requirements for leadership.

> Moreover it is required in stewards, that a man be found faithful. (1 Corinthians 4:2)

Faithfulness should not be motivated or defined by numbers, finances, or apparent success. In the parable of the talents, the lord said to the man who received five talents, "Well done, thou good and faithful servant: thou hast been **faithful** over a few things, I will make thee ruler over many things: enter thou into the joy of thy lord" (Matthew 25:21).

Show and Tell That Faithfulness Can Be What You Will Be Remembered for

Epaphras was Paul's friend. Four short verses tell us everything we know about this man. Sixty-nine words give us enough to not only want to know him, but to be like him. If someone wrote sixty-nine words about you, what would they write? What are you known for? For what will you be remembered?

1. A well-loved, faithful servant.

> As ye also learned of Epaphras our dear fellowservant, who is for you a faithful minister of Christ; who also declared unto us your love in the Spirit. (Colossians 1:7–8)

2. A local, hard-working, fervent, praying servant who knew and lived God's will for his life.

> Epaphras, who is one of you, a servant of Christ, saluteth you, always labouring fervently for you in prayers, that ye may stand perfect and complete in all the will of God. (Colossians 4:12)

3. A dear friend and prison inmate who suffered with Paul for the sake of the Gospel.

There salute thee Epaphras, my fellowprisoner in Christ Jesus. (Philemon 23)

Epaphras was one of Paul's best, most faithful friends. Wouldn't any of us want to be remembered as a faithful, well-loved, hard-working prayer warrior?

Show and Tell That Faithfulness Is Modeled by Our Faithful Lord

But the Lord is faithful, who shall stablish you, and keep you from evil. (2 Thessalonians 3:3)

People will disappoint you—but the Lord is faithful; friends will forget you—but the Lord is faithful; those you lean on for security will go a different direction in life—but the Lord is faithful; some of those you have looked up to will fall into sin—but the Lord is faithful; some friends will seemingly take away a piece of your heart—but the Lord is faithful. You will be disappointed in others, but you'll never be disappointed in the Lord. Why? The Lord is faithful!

A faithful God is worthy of belief and trust. A faithful God never wearies, never gets bored, never forgets, never changes. When God says, "I will," He will!

Faithful is he that calleth you, who also will do it. (1 Thessalonians 5:24)

This is a promise, a promise from a faithful Lord. God will strengthen **you** and establish **you** to do this—to be immovable, unshakeable, unwavering.

That we henceforth be no more children, tossed to and fro [easily distracted], and carried about with every wind of doctrine [don't let any imbalance in your theology knock you off balance in your passion for God and souls], by the sleight of men, and cunning craftiness, whereby they lie in wait to deceive; but speaking the truth in love, may grow

up into him in all things, which is the head, even Christ.
(Ephesians 4:14–15)

- What does it take to move you?
- Are you superglued to your time with God each day?
- Are you firmly fixed on what you will watch or not watch online or on screen?
- Are you immovable on your dating standards?
- Are you unshakeable in your prayer life?
- Are you unwavering in your thought life?

The Lord will keep you from all evil. (See Psalm 121:7.) The Lord taught us to pray, "deliver us from evil" in Matthew 6:13. And He *will* guard you and protect you. How?

With Divinely Appointed Hedges and Shields

Then Satan answered the Lord, and said, Doth Job fear God for nought? Hast not thou made an hedge about him, and about his house, and about all that he hath on every side? (Job 1:9–10)

For Thou, Lord, wilt bless the righteous; with favor wilt Thou compass him as with a shield. (Psalm 5:12)

With Divinely Appointed Governors

No temptation has overtaken you except such as is common to man; **but God is faithful**, who will not allow you to be tempted beyond what you are able, but with the temptation will also make the way of escape, that you may be able to bear it. (1 Corinthians 10:13 NKJV)

Therefore we do not lose heart. Even though our outward man is perishing, yet the inward man is being renewed day by day. For our **light affliction**, which is **but for a moment** [God puts a weight limit and a time limit on all our trials], is working for us a far more exceeding and eternal **weight** of glory, while we do not look at the **things which are seen**, but at the **things which are not seen**. For the things which are seen are **temporary**, but the things which are not seen are **eternal**. (2 Corinthians 4:16–18 NKJV)

With Divinely Appointed Angels

The angel of the Lord encampeth round about them that fear him, and delivereth them. (Psalm 34:7)

For He shall give his angels charge over thee, to keep thee in all thy ways. (Psalm 91:11)

My God hath sent his angel, and hath shut the lions' mouths, that they have not hurt me: forasmuch as before him innocency was found in me; and also before thee, O king, have I done no hurt. (Daniel 6:22)

Take heed that ye despise not one of these little ones; for I say unto you, That in heaven their angels do always behold the face of my Father which is in heaven [and you have to wonder what they see on that face when a little one is despised or offended]. (Matthew 18:10)

When God inspired the Psalmist to write *I*, *me*, and *my*, He had *you* in mind—not him, not her, not them, not it, but *you*!

I praise you, for I am fearfully and wonderfully made. Wonderful are your works; my soul knows it very well. My frame was not hidden from you, when I was being made in secret. . . . Your eyes saw my unformed substance; in Your book were written, every one of them, the days that were formed for me, . . . How precious to me are your thoughts, O God! How vast is the sum of them! If I would count them, they are more than the sand. I awake, and I am still with you. (Psalm 139:14–18 ESV)

The Lord will perfect that which concerneth me: thy mercy, O Lord, endureth for ever: forsake not the works of thine own hands. (Psalm 138:8)

The evil one is powerless in the presence of the Holy One of Israel.

- David prophesied of the Holy One of God.

For thou wilt not leave my soul in hell; neither wilt thou suffer thine Holy One to see corruption. (Psalm 16:10)

- Peter preached of the Holy One of God.

But ye denied the Holy One and the Just, and desired a murderer to be granted unto you. (Acts 3:14)

- The demons feared the Holy One of God.

Saying, Let us alone; what have we to do with thee, thou Jesus of Nazareth? art thou come to destroy us? I know thee who thou art, the Holy One of God. (Mark 1:24)

- The evil one will never again capture you.

And I give unto them eternal life; and they shall never perish, neither shall any man pluck them out of my hand. My Father, which gave them me, is greater than all; and no man is able to pluck them out of my Father's hand. (John 10:28–29)

- The evil one will never again control you.

Ye are of God, little children, and have overcome them: because greater is he that is in you, than he that is in the world. (1 John 4:4)

- The evil one will never again conquer you.

Nay, in all these things we are more than conquerors through him that loved us. For I am persuaded, that neither death, nor life, nor angels, nor principalities, nor powers, nor things present, nor things to come, nor height, nor depth, nor any other creature, shall be able to separate us from the love of God, which is in Christ Jesus our Lord. (Romans 8:37–39)

THE LAW OF SINCERITY

DANIEL 6:4–5

Neither was there any error or fault found in him. Then said these men, We shall not find any occasion against this Daniel, except we find it against him concerning the law of his God.

Show and Tell with Your Life the Kind of Sincerity That Pleases God

Sincerity is genuine character, free from hypocrisy, duplicity, or secret sins. Sincerity is doing what you should do because you want to and not because you have to. Sincerity begins with pure motives, grows through honest appraisals, and results in mature reality. Sincerity has no artificial flavors or counterfeit additives. Sincerity is pure and untarnished without spot, blemish, soil, or stain.

Show and Tell the Importance of Sincerity in Everyday Lives

In both the Old Testament and the New Testament we can find God-inspired events that will help us all to see the importance of genuine, transparent sincerity in our lives.

> Now therefore fear the Lord, and serve Him in sincerity and
> in truth: and put away the gods which your fathers served
> on the other side of the flood, and in Egypt; and serve ye
> the Lord. And if it seem evil unto you to serve the Lord,
> choose you this day whom ye will serve; whether the gods
> which your fathers served that were on the other side of the
> flood, or the gods of the Amorites, in whose land ye dwell:
> but as for me and my house, we will serve the Lord. (Joshua
> 24:14–15)

Make up your mind to be real. Don't pretend that you
want to serve the Lord, when you know that you would run
back to your Egyptian gods given the chance. Don't fake your
love for God, when the gods of the Amorites are much more
appealing to you. Be real! Make a choice. Man up! Decide
who you are going to love and then love. Decide who you
want to serve and then serve. There is not enough time in life
to halt between decisions.

If you want stress in your life (the kind of stress that
makes you feel like you are being tortured on a Roman
stretcher), then attempt to please both God *and* your friends,
or God *and* your flesh. It is a miserable, lonely, disappointing
way to live.

The secret motivation here is fear. A fear of man brings
a snare that entraps you to the assumed wishes of others.
Those who fear what others think, forget that most others
don't think, and if they do, it is usually about themselves and
not you. If you care what others think about you, it is just a
matter of time before you realize that they really don't care
about you at all!

I'll say it again: the secret motivation here is fear. A
healthy and heartfelt fear and respect for God is the greatest
motivation for a life of sincerity. It is the only way to be real,
because you are real. Fear God. Respect His holiness. Dread
displeasing Him. Hate what He hates. Love what He loves. Be
constantly aware of His presence. Be overwhelmed with His
power, His sovereignty, His strength, and His majesty.

The true fear of the Lord is not shaking in your boots at the potential consequences of your sin, but trembling at His Word with the dread of displeasing or disappointing such a powerful, yet caring God.

Make up your mind to be real. If you lived in Joshua's house, and wanted to stay there, you would want to serve your Lord in sincerity and truth. No questions asked.

Have you ever felt invisible? Have you ever felt like no one even notices you or cares if you exist? Do you sometimes feel like the Lone Ranger—without Tonto by your side?

Much can be seen through a window of eight panes. There are only eight verses from John's writings that clue us in to Nathanael's character.

> Philip findeth Nathanael, and saith unto him, We have found him, of whom Moses in the law, and the prophets, did write, Jesus of Nazareth, the son of Joseph. And Nathanael said unto him, Can there any good thing come out of Nazareth? Philip saith unto him, Come and see. Jesus saw Nathanael coming to Him, and saith of him, Behold an Israelite indeed, in whom is no guile! Nathanael saith unto Him, Whence knowest Thou me? Jesus answered and said unto him, Before that Philip called thee, when thou wast under the fig tree, I saw thee. Nathanael answered and saith unto him, Rabbi, thou art the Son of God; thou art the King of Israel. Jesus answered and said unto him, Because I said unto thee, I saw thee under the fig tree, believest thou? thou shalt see greater things than these. And he saith unto him, Verily, verily, I say unto you, Hereafter ye shall see heaven open, and the angels of God ascending and descending upon the Son of man. (John 1:45–51)

> There were together Simon Peter, and Thomas called Didymus, and Nathanael of Cana in Galilee, and the sons of Zebedee, and two other of his disciples. (John 21:2)

If only eight verses, seven sentences, or two hundred words were said about you, what would they be? Here is a man who was chosen to closely follow Christ for three years, whose name will be on one of the foundations of the New Jerusalem, who faithfully served His Lord and King and was martyred in doing so, and whose whole life is explained in eight short verses!

John, the beloved apostle, has a way of bringing the unknown out of oblivion. Matthew, Mark, and Luke name this apostle Bartholomew. John got to know Nathanael (Bartholomew) in a much more personal way. And we benefit from John's writing.

Even though Nathanael is not well known, he was and is well known by the one who matters—our wonderful Lord. And listen to what Scripture says about this so called *invisible* apostle.

Nathanael. He was the real deal. Jesus said so. I would love for Jesus to say about me what He said about Nathanael. Maybe someday. Jesus looks right past our attempts to look young, to look fit, or to look good. His eyes are far superior to any CAT scan, X-ray, or heart scope. He looks right into our spiritual hearts and knows what we are, what we do, and why we do it. The first time Nathanael met Jesus, Jesus greeted him with the words, "Now, here is a true Israelite—a man of complete integrity! No deceit. No pretense. No guile. A genuine son of Israel." This freaked Nathanael out. How did this man know him? Nathanael had never met Him before. Did Philip give Jesus his bio? So he asked the simple question, "How do you know me?" He got a simple answer. "Because I have been meeting with you every morning in your favorite devotion spot . . . you know, under the shade of the fig tree! Great place to meet. Few distractions. Nobody else is up at that time in the morning."

Philip knew where to find Nathanael. Good friends usually know their friends' habits. The Lord knew where Nathanael had been. Unknown to Nathanael, Jesus, by His Spirit, had met him there many times before.

For many people in Palestine, the fig tree was a kind of private room. The fig tree grows to a height of about fifteen feet but its branches spread out as far as twenty-five feet. It was a custom to have a fig tree near the door of a cottage. In Palestine, many of the houses, especially the poorer ones, only had one room, so if someone sought a quiet place to pray or meditate, they often went to the privacy of the shade of the fig tree.

It was as if Jesus said, "Nathanael, I saw you in prayer and meditation in your secret place, your secret closet. And not only did I see your secret devotion, I also saw the secrets of your heart."

Do you have a *secret holy place* where you meet Jesus in a consistent way? Do your family and friends know where you are and what you are doing?

Does the song "Holy Place" convict your heart?

> There is a holy place far from the rapid pace
> where I seek face to face, my God and King.
> I must go every day, and that without delay,
> to read His Word and pray and praises bring.
>
> The Word of God will light the darkest path,
> Its treasures flow with strength anew.
> Help me to hide its words within my heart;
> Take this hour, make me more like You![1]

Does the song "Quiet Time" stir your conscience?

> Before I start each day, there is a special place
> I love to go alone and seek my Savior's face:
> I find wisdom in His Word to instruct me in His will,
> And I hear His gentle voice say, "My child, be still."
>
> He's with me all the time, wherever I may go;
> Each moment of the day, He's always there I know.
> But I need that special time when I bow before His throne,
> Just to read His Word and talk with my Lord alone.

> My quiet time alone gives me power to obey,
> My quiet time alone with God each day.
> I talk to Him in prayer; ev'ry day He meets me there,
> My quiet time alone with God.[2]

Your sincerity should mean as much to you as it does to God. Be real. Be genuine. Sincerely love your God. Sincerely live for Him.

Show and Tell the Importance of Godly Sincerity and a Clear Testimony

Most adults know that young people can scope out a phony a thousand miles away. If you are to be a lion-like leader whose influence impacts your peers, you must desire to have a life's testimony that mirrors the testimony of the apostle Paul. Here is what he said toward the end of his life.

> For our rejoicing [boasting, proud confidence] is this, the testimony of our conscience [I can give my testimony with confidence and a clear conscience], that in simplicity [simple, pure motives; single-mindedly serving with no ulterior motives] and godly sincerity [pure, unsoiled, and free from spot or blemish to such a degree as to bear examination in full sunlight], not with fleshly wisdom, but by the grace of God [This is not magic. No pills can do this for anyone. I did not finally figure out with a fleshly, itsy-bitsy mind how to do this. Such single-minded, godly sincerity can come only from God's divine enablement, which is available to me if I stay humble before God.], we have had our conversation in the world [our unbelieving friends saw that we behaved with sincerity and simplicity], and more abundantly to you-ward [even more with you where we focused most of our time and attention]. (2 Corinthians 1:12)

The simplicity of godly sincerity is simply wonderful. It thrills a heart, encourages others, and runs through life with no regrets. It is the only way to look back at your year in

December, your career at your retirement, or even your life as you approach its end with confidence and a clear conscience that you, by the enabling grace of God, lived a godly, honest, unhypocritical life. Paul bragged on God who enabled him by His grace to live an exemplary life. Our goal, like Paul, should be to live a God-honoring life with nothing to hide.

The word *sincere* comes from a root word that is best illustrated with the phrase "without wax." Some deceiving merchants would take a cracked clay pot, fill the cracks with a colored wax, and try to sell it as if it were perfect. If the buyer would hold the pot up to the sun, the cracks would be exposed, proving that the clay pot was inferior or *insincere.*

How many of us could pray, "Lord, help me. I am yours and I try to keep my body (my vessel) clean and together. But I have cracks! Although I try to conceal them by keeping my good side out, I am nothing more than a cracked pot. If anyone looks too closely they are going to be disappointed."

As the only wise, eternal Inspector holds your vessel (your clay pot) up to the sunlight, what does He see?

"Looks good. Nice coloring. Shaped a little funny in some places. Sturdy. Oh! What's this? A crack filled with wax to try to hide that it is there? Your anger has been getting the best of you lately, huh? Oh, another crack? Another late night online being unfaithful to your future wife in your mind? Look here. Here's another crack. You had only two days of meaningful devotions within the past two weeks? And look here. My, why would you get with your friends and judge, attack, or belittle another brother in Christ who is serving Me faithfully? And there is one more little crack. It looks like you are having a tough time in your consistent walk with Me."

Is it possible that the Inspector puts the clay pot down and looks for another to use with fewer cracks? We can disqualify ourselves from spiritual leadership by ignoring God's warnings and walking into sin.

Are you a synonym or an antonym to biblical sincerity? Which of the following terms most describes your private life when it is just you—or, I should say, just you and God?

- Synonyms—Are you pure, guileless, without evil, true, genuine, real, unconcealed, or cleansed?

- Antonyms—Are you hypocritical, false, deceitful, insincere, fake, or phony?

THE LAW OF LONELINESS

DANIEL 6:6–9

Then these presidents and princes assembled together to the king, and said thus unto him, King Darius, live forever. All [This is a lie. All but Daniel.] the presidents of the kingdom, the governors, and the princes, the counselors, and the captains, have consulted together to establish a royal statute, and to make a firm decree, that whosoever shall ask a petition of any God or man for thirty days, save of thee, O king, he shall be cast into the den of lions. Now, O king, establish the decree, and sign the writing, that it be not changed, according to the law of the Medes and Persians, which altereth not. Wherefore king Darius signed the writing and the decree.

Show and Tell with Your Life the Kind of Loneliness That Accompanies Leadership

The odds were not in Daniel's favor—122 to 1. And he was the one. His coworkers were bound and determined to get rid of him.

He hadn't seen his family since he was kidnapped and taken as a fifteen-year old POW to Babylon. As far as he knew, his family was murdered during the siege and takeover of Jerusalem by Nebuchadnezzar. His three best friends—Hananiah, Mishael, and Azariah—had silently disappeared. (We assume that they did not possess the longevity of Daniel's eighty-plus years.) He was not invited to Belshazzar's party. There is no record that Daniel ever married. Daniel was a lonely man.

> He [Jesus] came unto his own, and his own received him not. (John 1:11)

Leaders are no strangers to loneliness. Constant rejection is a direct result of taking a consistent stand.

> He [Jesus] is despised and rejected of men; a man of sorrows, and acquainted with grief: and we hid as it were our faces from him; he was despised, and we esteemed him not. (Isaiah 53:3)

If compromising God's Word is the only way to keep a copilot, leaders are willing to fly solo.

> I am become a stranger unto my brethren, and an alien unto my mother's children. (Psalm 69:8)

Leaders know that rejection, ridicule, backstabbing, gossip, scorn, and derision are just part of their daily schedules. Leadership can be extremely lonely at times.

Show and Tell That Loneliness Was Christ's Constant Companion

Are you lonely? Do you feel like you don't fit in with anyone? Do you feel like there are hardly any other Christians in your school and those who say they are Christians live worse than those who don't even pretend to be saved? Do you feel that you are going to be lonely for the rest of your life?

Life can be tough. Many who take a stand for Christ wrestle with loneliness. We must remember that life is short and eternity is sure. We are getting a little taste of what Jesus experienced on earth. Our Savior walked in loneliness. One of the saddest documentaries of His life on earth He explained to a scribe who thought he was willing to be a disciple and follow Christ, "Foxes have holes and birds of the air have nests, but the Son of Man has nowhere to lay His head" (Mathew 8:20 NKJV). A fox has little use or purpose on earth other than survival, yet he has a hole to crawl into where his tiny brood waits to snuggle up against him for warmth.

Even pesky little birds have claimed their territory, built their home, gathered food, started a family, and have little chirpers waiting for them to come feed them and protect them. Jesus had no such hole or nest. He did have friends (and still does), but most of those friends could not have survived the same dark and lonely path that Christ walked for us.

Humanly speaking, Jesus was a lonely man.

> For he grew up before him like a young plant, and like a root out of dry ground; he had no form or majesty that we should look at him, and no beauty that we should desire him. He was despised and rejected by men; a man of sorrows, and acquainted with grief; and as one from whom men hide their faces he was despised, and we esteemed him not.
>
> Surely he has borne our griefs and carried our sorrows; yet we esteemed him stricken, smitten by God, and afflicted. (Isaiah 53:2–4 ESV)

Just a few hours before Christ was crucified, He was arrested by a mob of hateful men armed with swords and clubs and led by Judas Iscariot. When Christ could have been comforted by twelve men surrounding Him or even three of His closest followers or even one that truly loved Him, He stood all alone. "All the disciples forsook him, and fled" (Matthew 26:56). Of course, you could say that Jesus was used to this by now, because even at His birth His mother Mary "wrapped him in swaddling clothes, and laid him in a manger; because there was no room for them in the inn" (Luke 2:7). Although a stranger on earth, our Lord was no stranger to loneliness.

There are two ways to cope with loneliness. One is rooted in an awareness of God's presence and the other in an alertness to other's needs. Leadership may have its lonely moments, but such loneliness can be overshadowed by a focus on God and others. Just as an ingrown toenail can cause pain and discomfort in your toe, so can ingrown eyeballs cause pain and discomfort to your soul.

As a child of God you are never truly alone. As a servant of God you can always find someone to serve.

The first secret in dealing with loneliness is an awareness of God's presence. Jesus, although humanly speaking seemed to live a lonely life, said "I am not alone" and "he that sent me is with me: the Father hath not left me alone; for I do always those things that please him" (John 8:16, 29).

Paul not only knew loneliness, but the reassuring and promised presence of God standing with him.

> At my first defense no one stood with me, but all forsook me. May it not be charged against them.

> But the Lord stood with me and strengthened me, so that the message might be preached fully through me, and that all the Gentiles might hear. Also I was delivered out of the mouth of the lion. And the Lord will deliver me from every evil work and preserve me for His heavenly kingdom. To Him be glory forever and ever. Amen! (2 Timothy 4:16–18 NKJV)

I love Paul's prayer to Timothy.

> The Lord Jesus Christ be with your spirit. Grace be with you. Amen. (2 Timothy 4:22 NKJV)

Time for some good meditation. Slowly, carefully, and thoughtfully read out loud the verses that I have listed below. Stop at each punctuation mark and think. God's living Word can cut right to the core of our loneliness. I promise.

> Let your conversation be without covetousness; and be content with such things as ye have: for He hath said, I will never leave thee, nor forsake thee. (Hebrews 13:5)

> Go ye therefore, and teach all nations, baptizing them in the name of the Father, and of the Son, and of the Holy Ghost: teaching them to observe all things whatsoever I have commanded you: and, lo, I am with you alway, even unto the end of the world. Amen. (Matthew 28:19–20)

> That Christ may dwell in your hearts by faith. (Ephesians 3:17)

> Be strong and of a good courage, fear not, nor be afraid of them: for the Lord thy God, he it is that doth go with thee; he will not fail thee, nor forsake thee. (Deuteronomy 31:6)

There shall not any man be able to stand before thee all the days of thy life: as I was with Moses, so I will be with thee: I will not fail thee, nor forsake thee. (Joshua 1:5)

Fear thou not; for I am with thee: be not dismayed; for I am thy God: I will strengthen thee; yea, I will help thee; yea, I will uphold thee with the right hand of my righteousness. (Isaiah 41:10)

God understood the need and desire for companionship before Adam even had a companion. God said, "It is not good that the man should be alone; I will make him an help meet for him" (Genesis 2:18). In speaking of friendly accountability Solomon wrote, "Two are better than one; because they have a good reward for their labour. For if they fall, the one will lift up his fellow: but woe to him that is alone when he falleth; for he hath not another to help him up" (Ecclesiastes 4:9–10).

God will take care of us and help us overcome this loneliness.

THE LAW OF HUMILITY

DANIEL 6:10

Now when Daniel knew that the writing was signed, he went into his house; and his windows being open in his chamber toward Jerusalem, **he kneeled upon his knees** three times a day.

Show and Tell with Your Life the Kind of Humility That Pleases God

Humility recognizes that God and others are actually responsible for your achievements in life.

But he giveth more grace. Wherefore he saith, God resisteth the proud, but giveth grace unto the humble. (James 4:6)

Humility understands the concept of voluntarily placing yourself on the lowest level by willingly submitting to all others.

Though the Lord be high, yet hath he respect unto the lowly: but the proud he knoweth afar off. (Psalm 138:6)

Humility comes in many colors.

- humility of dress = modesty
- humility of knowledge = discretion
- humility of communication = limited and careful online presence; etc.

A man's pride shall bring him low: but honour shall uphold the humble in spirit. (Proverbs 29:23)

Humility means you know your inabilities and inadequacies and therefore depend totally on the enabling grace of God.

Show and Tell That There Is a Constant Battle Between Pride and Humility

Humility is like a desert mirage. Just about the time you see it and think you have arrived, an overwhelming realization of our own selfishness and pride takes over. True humility looks into the past and sees what God and others have accomplished, lives in the present with recognition of its total dependence on God, and views the future with fear of failure without the enabling grace of God and encouraging support of others.

As a selfish man striving for humility, I think about me way too often and too long. Without humility I forfeit the grace of God in my life. Without humility I walk in the weakness of my own flesh. Without humility I cannot comfortably yoke up with my Lord Jesus Christ. Without humility I cannot fulfill God's purpose for my life and existence of daily watching God conform me into a likeness, image, or icon of His Son. Without humility I struggle with anger, lust, fear, and arrogance. Without humility I drive others away from God rather than draw them closer to Him. Without humility I will never succeed in this life.

So what do you do? How do you ever find victory? This is where the Ephesians 4 plan applies once again: put off, renew your mind, and put on. My part is to stop pride whenever I recognize it and to do whatever I can to *think biblically* when selfishness attacks.

Daniel was forced to defy authorities in his life but did so with an attitude of meekness and humility motivated by a genuine concern for those who were opposing him.

> He [Daniel] requested of the prince of the eunuchs. (Daniel 1:8)

Daniel did not demand his rights. He did not pitch a fit or start a blog; he simply made a request. When you question an authority's decision or direction never be afraid to ask questions with a kind, nonabrasive, humble spirit.

> Now God had brought Daniel into favour and tender love with the prince of the eunuchs. (Daniel 1:9)

> "Please test your servants for ten days, and let them give us vegetables to eat and water to drink. Then let our appearance be examined before you, and the appearance of the young men who eat the portion of the king's delicacies; and as you see fit, so deal with your servants." (Daniel 1:12–13 NKJV)

No one is challenged or undermined with the attitude of "Let's try something. If it works, great. If not, then you can do what you think is best." It creates an opportunity for God to show Himself strong. When you cannot understand your dad or mom's rule, instead of pouting or shouting, a simple question can respectfully be asked. "Mom, I know that you've done this before, but have you thought about trying it this way?" "Dad, would you let me try doing this a different way for one week? If my way doesn't work, fine, we can go back to your plan."

> Then Daniel answered with counsel and wisdom to Arioch the captain of the king's guard, which was gone forth to slay the wise men of Babylon: he answered and said to Arioch the king's captain, Why is the decree so hasty from the king? Then Arioch made the thing known to Daniel. (Daniel 2:14–15)

Daniel answered. It was not a hasty answer; it was not a smart-mouthed answer; it was not a "what do *you* know" answer; it was not an "I don't agree with you, so I don't have to listen to you" answer; it was an answer wrapped in godly counsel and heavenly wisdom.

Daniel answered with *counsel* (discernment and prudence) and *wisdom* (discretion and judgment). What leader would not want to be approached with a wise, thoughtful, discerning question? It is not always *what* is said but the *way* that it is said that brings about peace or strife. True, biblical wisdom is described by James as being pure, peaceable, gentle, considerate, approachable, open to reason, easily entreated, full of mercy, full of good fruits, productive, impartial, and sincere. Such a list of characteristics is foreign to a proud person. Wise humility studies both sides of the issue before it ever opens its mouth. If 2 Timothy 2:15 is heeded, 2 Timothy 2:24–26 can become a reality.

> Study to shew thyself approved unto God, a workman that needeth not to be ashamed, rightly dividing the word of truth. (2 Timothy 2:15)

> The servant of the Lord must not strive; but be gentle unto all men, apt to teach, patient, in meekness instructing those that oppose themselves; if God peradventure will give them repentance to the acknowledging of the truth; and that they may recover themselves out of the snare of the devil, who are taken captive by him at his will. (2 Timothy 2:24–26)

People remember what we are long after they forget what we have said. Ask yourself some hard questions, and then be honest with your answers.

- Am I approachable?
- Do I attempt to be understanding?
- Can those who are not sure where they stand come to me for counsel without fear of being viewed as a worldly compromiser?
- Am I known for my harshness or my gentleness?

Strife comes from those who strive. It makes little difference whether it is with the fists, your tongues, or a blog, it is still contentious, harsh, unloving strife. Once your friends know that you really care for them, then they will be ready to follow your leadership.

> So Daniel went in and asked the king to give him time, that he might tell the king the interpretation. Then Daniel went to his house, and made the decision known to Hananiah, Mishael, and Azariah, his companions, that they might seek mercies from the God of heaven concerning this secret, so that Daniel and his companions might not perish with the rest of the wise men of Babylon. (Daniel 2:16–18 NKJV)

> "I thank You and praise You, O God of my fathers; You have given me wisdom and might, and have now made known to me what we asked of You, for You have made known to us the king's demand." (Daniel 2:23 NKJV)

> Daniel answered in the presence of the king, and said, "The secret which the king has demanded, the wise men, the astrologers, the magicians, and the soothsayers cannot declare to the king. But there is a God in heaven who reveals secrets, and He has made known to King Nebuchadnezzar what will be in the latter days. (Daniel 2:27–28)

The secret of humility is often found in the prayer closet. Where there is little humility, there is little prayer. Where there is little prayer, there is little humility. Without humility in prayer there will be little humility in the pulpit. God dependence is mentored in private but observed in public.

Daniel was faced with a life or death situation and what did he do? He got his friends together for a prayer meeting. His first response to his trouble was to run to God in prayer.

Daniel asked (he did not demand) for a little time. Time for what? Time to pray. Even though the king would not understand, that was Daniel's standard operating procedure. Daniel went to his special hiding place, his place of prayer, his own upper room closet. Daniel asked his friends to seek mercies from God. As soon as the secret was revealed to Daniel, what did he do? If you are thinking that he sent a quick text or posted on Facebook to his friends, you are wrong. He did not even run to the king who could stay his execution. He went back to God and thanked Him for giving wisdom.

Daniel made sure to emphasize that no astrologer, magician, soothsayer, or wise man (even himself) could reveal the king's secret. Daniel's humility went to the source of the answered prayer—God. He did not share the story in such a way that he was the heroic prayer warrior, but wanted all to focus on God.

> Then Daniel answered and said before the king, Let thy gifts be to thyself, and give thy rewards to another; yet I will read the writing unto the king, and make known to him the interpretation. (Daniel 5:17)

Daniel humbly did his job without expecting or even accepting any personal gifts or recognition. He did not need to be third in the kingdom; he was content to be Daniel—God's ambassador to Babylon.

> O thou king, the most high God gave Nebuchadnezzar thy father a kingdom, and majesty, and glory, and honour: and for the majesty that He gave him, all people, nations, and languages, trembled and feared before him: whom he would he slew; and whom he would he kept alive; and whom he would he set up; and whom he would he put down. But when his heart was lifted up, and his mind hardened in pride, he was deposed from his kingly throne, and they took his glory from him: and he was driven from the sons of men; and his heart was made like the beasts, and his dwelling was with the wild asses: they fed him with grass like oxen, and his body was wet with the dew of heaven; till he knew that the most high God ruled in the kingdom of men, and that he appointeth over it whomsoever he will. And thou his son, O Belshazzar, hast not humbled thine heart, though thou knewest all this; but hast lifted up thyself against the Lord

of heaven; and they have brought the vessels of His house before thee, and thou, and thy lords, thy wives, and thy concubines, have drunk wine in them; and thou hast praised the gods of silver, and gold, of brass, iron, wood, and stone, which see not, nor hear, nor know: and the God in whose hand thy breath is, and whose are all thy ways, hast thou not glorified. (Daniel 5:18–23)

Daniel lived in the midst of a proud kingdom. He served proud men and saw the devastation and the consequences of pride. No matter how important man seems to be, God can and will quickly bring those with such haughty hearts crashing down to such devastation that there is nothing left to be proud about. Then, in desperation, they still are thinking about themselves and cry for mercy to be free from the pain and consequences they have brought about through their arrogance towards God. Long before Peter and James penned the words, Daniel knew that God resisted the proud and gave grace only to the humble.

THE LAW OF PRAYERFULNESS

—————————•—————————

DANIEL 6:10

Now when Daniel knew that the writing was signed, he went into his house; and his windows being open in his chamber toward Jerusalem, he kneeled upon his knees three times a day, and **prayed**.

Show and Tell with Your Life the Kind of Prayerfulness That Pleases God

Not even a den of hungry lions could deter Daniel from praying. To lead others closer to God, a leader must know how to talk to God. A wise leader is in the habit of asking God for wisdom. Many godly leaders know both the power and the necessity of prayer.

And Solomon said, Thou hast shewed unto thy servant David my father great mercy, according as he walked before thee in truth, and in righteousness, and in uprightness of heart with thee; and thou hast kept for him this great kindness, that thou hast given him a son to sit on his throne, as it is this day. And now, O Lord my God, thou hast made thy servant king instead of David my father: and I am but a little child: I know not how to go out or come in. And thy servant is in the midst of thy people which thou hast chosen, a great people, that cannot be numbered nor counted for multitude. Give therefore thy servant an understanding heart to judge thy people, that I may discern between good and bad:

for who is able to judge this thy so great a people? And the speech pleased the Lord, that Solomon had asked this thing. And God said unto him, Because thou hast asked this thing, and hast not asked for thyself long life; neither hast asked riches for thyself, nor hast asked the life of thine enemies; but hast asked for thyself understanding to discern judgment; Behold, I have done according to thy words: lo, I have given thee a wise and an understanding heart; so that there was none like thee before thee, neither after thee shall any arise like unto thee. And I have also given thee that which thou hast not asked, both riches, and honour: so that there shall not be any among the kings like unto thee all thy days. (1 Kings 3:6–13)

Show and Tell That a Careful Leader Is Always a Prayerful Leader

Now therefore, O our God, hear the prayer of thy servant, and his supplications, and cause thy face to shine upon thy sanctuary that is desolate, for the Lord's sake. O my God, incline Thine ear, and hear; open thine eyes, and behold our desolations, and the city which is called by thy name: for we do not present our supplications before thee for our righteousnesses, but for thy great mercies. O Lord, hear; O Lord, forgive; O Lord, hearken and do; defer not, for thine own sake, O my God: for thy city and thy people are called by thy name. (Daniel 9:17–19)

God directly answered the prayers of Daniel and his three friends when they "desired mercies" from the Father of mercies. God can and will still do that today.

Then Daniel went to his house, and made the thing known to Hananiah, Mishael, and Azariah, his companions, that they would desire mercies of the God of heaven concerning this secret; that Daniel and his fellows should not perish with the rest of the wise men of Babylon. Then was the secret revealed unto Daniel in a night vision. Then Daniel blessed the God of heaven (Daniel 2:17–19).

It is probable that Solomon's Proverbs had a huge impact on Daniel's life. Daniel established the habit of "crying out to God" for wisdom and knowledge whenever he was in need.

Yea, if thou criest after knowledge, and liftest up thy voice for understanding; if thou seekest her as silver, and searchest for her as for hid treasures; then shalt thou understand the fear of the Lord, and find the knowledge of God. For the Lord giveth wisdom: out of His mouth cometh knowledge and understanding. (Proverbs 2:3–6)

Lion-like leaders pray. Daniel prayed. God gave Daniel, Hananiah, Mishael, and Azariah wisdom when they needed it most. Can we not assume that what God did then He still promises to do today? God gave them knowledge and skill in all learning and wisdom.

If any of you lack wisdom, let him ask of God. (James 1:5)

God knew that when He answered one of Daniel's prayers, Daniel would run back to Him to thank Him and praise Him for the answer. Daniel not only knew how to pray for things, he knew how to be thankful for the things that God gave.

I thank thee, and praise thee, O thou God of my fathers, who hast given me wisdom and might, and hast made known unto me now what we desired of thee: for thou hast now made known unto us the king's matter. (Daniel 2:23)

Daniel went to his prayer chamber and prayed even in the face of a lions' den.

Now when Daniel knew that the writing was signed, he went into his house. (Daniel 6:10)

What if that same decree were given this month? How would it affect us? How would it affect our churches?

Since there are no lions' dens to scare us into silence before God, why are we so silent? What if we had to pay for the privilege of praying—for unlimited access to God—as we pay for the use of our phones and other devices? Would we be willing to take on the monthly cost? Would we communicate with God as we much as we do with our Verizon Friends? Would we ever be charged for excessive texts or going over our allotment of minutes with God?

What would it take to stop *you* from praying as Daniel did? Money? A new phone or tablet? The promise of a relationship? A new car? What?

What *keeps* you from praying consistently as Daniel did? A lack of concern? A lack of effort? A shallow relationship with Jesus Christ? Your peers? Social media? Video games? What?

What was the big deal about Daniel's windows being open?

> . . . and his windows being open in his chamber toward Jerusalem (Daniel 6:10)

God can hear you through the walls, can't He? Doesn't the Bible say you are supposed to hide in your closet with the doors closed and pray? Daniel's open windows were not for show and were not to make a statement that he was much more spiritual than others. His open windows were one small way to praise Jehovah God in that pagan culture; they were one small way to show a hostile world how important his holy God was to him.

I think many would say, "I can be like Daniel. I can march right up to that prayer chamber and pray to God with my windows wide open!" But then I wonder if you keep the windows open in your school dining halls? At restaurants? In your church by bowing your head and involving yourself in corporate prayer? Don't shut the windows of prayer to God and the windows of blessing from God. Open your windows; don't hide the fact that you talk to God.

Daniel 6:10 tells us that Daniel "kneeled upon his knees three times a day, and prayed." He kneeled, even in his eighties. While you don't have to kneel, it does not hurt to kneel. If you cannot concentrate while seated or standing, kneel.

You should never kneel for others to see your habits, but you kneel for God to see your heart. I heard someone say that the *position* of your body can often express the *condition* of your heart. Have you ever been so burdened about something that while praying in your room, without even thinking about it, you knelt next to your bed and poured your heart out to God?

Daniel knelt three times a day! When I think about my schedule, I can't imagine. Daniel must have been a busy man. But even though he was the prime minister of the Medo-Persian Empire, he kept his schedule clear for prayer.

Daniel did not pray like most of us—just when we get in trouble, in a jam, or need something really quick.

> [Daniel] prayed, and gave thanks before his God, as he did aforetime. (Daniel 6:10)

It was Daniel's habit of life! It was part of his character to pray.

We all need to thank God more than we do. The best biblical way to send a prayerful thank you note to God is found in Ephesians 5:20.

> Giving thanks always for all things unto God and the Father in the name of our Lord Jesus Christ.

It looks like a continuous and repeated action is being emphasized here. It is thanks given always, at all times, perpetually, over and over, continuously, and forever. This is the total package, not just the parts you like but all in its entirety. Thanks-giving must have a recipient—the Father—who has done something to generate a thankful heart. Meditate on God as your loving, heavenly Father and you will have more to be thankful for than you have minutes in a day. The blessings of eternal life and the benefits of abundant life all come through Jesus Christ and what He has done for us, therefore, all thanksgiving should return through Him in prayer.

> Now therefore, O our God, hear the prayer of thy servant,
> and his supplications, and cause thy face to shine upon thy
> sanctuary that is desolate, for the Lord's sake. (Daniel 9:17)

Daniel knew how to keep his focus off himself and direct
it to God and others. Other than Daniel's purposeful character, his faithfulness to his convictions, and his consistency
and fervency in prayer, it was his concern for God's people
(others) that motivated this octogenarian to live the holy and
happy life that he lived.

His prayer was full of Scripture. Much of what he prayed
came from the old manuscript that Jeremiah wrote, which
Daniel must have read, meditated on, and wept over. His
prayer was from a humble heart. If you read the context, you
can see that the sackcloth, fasting, and ashes were symbolic to
the true condition of Daniel's heart.

> O my God, incline thine ear, and hear; open thine eyes, and
> behold our desolations, and the city which is called by thy
> name: for we do not present our supplications before thee for
> our righteousnesses, but for thy great mercies. (Daniel 9:18)

His prayer included a zeal for God's glory. He wanted all
to see God's great mercies in the way that God answered his
prayers. It was all about God and not him.

Daniel prayed for the impossible. Jerusalem was in ruins;
Judah's sin was excessive; God's people were scattered and
enslaved. But Daniel knew that God was in control of both
kings and kingdoms. If God is in control of entire kingdoms,
it is silly to think that He cannot control our lives.

> O Lord, hear; O Lord, forgive; O Lord, hearken and do; defer
> not, for thine own sake, O my God: for thy city and thy peo-
> ple are called by thy name. (Daniel 9:19)

His prayer was earnest as we can see in the way he repeated the words "O Lord." We really don't know why Daniel
repeated the Lord's name three times, but we do know that
this was not vain repetition. Maybe Daniel did not sense
his closeness to God and it was a thoughtful, needful crying

out to God to sense His presence. Or maybe his own heart was being overcome with unworthiness as he prayed to his all-powerful heavenly Father.

We should not pray just for God's blessings, but for the very presence of God. We shouldn't want God's Spirit just to be with us, but glad to be with us, comfortable in being with us, and eager to do His work in our lives.

THE LAW OF THANKFULNESS
————————•————————

DANIEL 6:10
. . . and gave thanks before his God.

Show and Tell with Your Life the Kind of Thankfulness That Pleases God

Spiritual leaders are Spirit filled and Spirit controlled, and they specialize in "giving thanks always for all things" (Ephesians 5:20).

Covetousness is the archenemy of contentment. When will we be thankful for what God has already given us rather than craving more and more? At what point in life will we be truly thankful?

High-level leaders know how to enter into the presence of royalty; they enter the "gates with thanksgiving" and the "courts with praise" (Psalm 100:4).

If you are not thankful for what you already have, you probably will not be thankful for what you will receive.

In everything give thanks: for this is the will of God in Christ Jesus concerning you (1 Thessalonians 5:18).

God gave you 86,400 seconds today. Have you used one to say "thank you?"[1]

There is no such thing as gratitude unexpressed. If it is unexpressed, it is plain, old-fashioned ingratitude.[2]

Most human beings have an almost infinite capacity for taking things for granted.[3]

Feeling gratitude and not expressing it is like wrapping a present and not giving it.[4]

Giving thanks always for all things unto God and the Father in the name of our Lord Jesus Christ. (Ephesians 5:20)

Show and Tell That It Is Better to Thank God for What He Has Done, Than to Worry About What He May or May Not Do

Don't worry about anything. Pray about everything! Instead of allowing worry to consume your thoughts, learn to thank God for anything and everything you can think of. Begin, continue, and finish your prayers with thanksgiving. While you are in the midst of thanksgiving, give your requests to God. Instead of worrying about what might happen in the future, spend the same amount of time and energy thanking God for what has happened in the past.

Be careful for nothing; but in everything by prayer and supplication with thanksgiving let your requests be made known unto God. (Philippians 4:6)

Any of God's commands and promises that have anything to do with prayer have everything to do with *100% words*. Ephesians 5:20 says to give thanks "*always* for all things," Hebrews 13:15 reminds us to praise *continually*, and Philippians 4:6 teaches us to worry about *nothing* but pray about *everything*. 1 Thessalonians 5:17 tells us to "pray without ceasing" and to give thanks for *everything*. David writes in Psalm 62:8 to trust "at *all times*."

Worry is not contagious but can be learned very quickly. It is much easier to worry than to trust. It is easier to fear than to thank. Got a problem with worrying? Start with Philippians 4:6–7. Continue with Philippians 4:8. And find the victory in Philippians 4:9.

Pray. Think. Do!

Prayer is the first step of three to crush anxious care and pulverize paralyzing worry.

Pray. Think. Do!

Show and Tell That It Doesn't Seem to Be Much of a Sacrifice to Offer a Sacrifice of Praise

In a world hostile to Christianity, it is becoming increasingly more difficult to share your faith with others, especially in the work place. To honor your employer in a work culture that may not be Christ friendly, witness the "13:15" way—that is, the Hebrews 13:15 way.

> Through Jesus, therefore, let us continually offer to God a sacrifice of praise—the fruit of lips that openly profess his name. (NIV)

Sharing your faith the 13:15 way is much easier than you may think. One of the best ways to acknowledge God's presence and power to unbelievers is to share with them (confess to them) what God has been doing in your life. Listen to the verse again: "Through Jesus, therefore, let us continually offer to God a sacrifice of praise—the fruit of lips that openly profess his name."

Simply share how good God is without mentioning how bad they are. Don't freak here. I know that repentance is essential to salvation, and we are saved *from* our sins. But I also know that "the goodness of God leads you to repentance" (Romans 2:4 NKJV). My prayer is that when unbelievers see that I believe in a good God, then sometime when we connect outside of work, they will ask me about my good God.

Don't forget about the "sacrifice" aspect of Hebrews 13:15—"Through Jesus." Remember, Jesus was the final, once-and-for-all sacrifice. So as Christians—though we are free from offering living, animal sacrifices on an altar—we are to offer ourselves as a living sacrifice. We are to continually praise and thank God for His goodness within earshot of both believers (so they can be comforted) and unbelievers (so they can be convicted).

Since Jesus was the final sacrifice, we need offer no more Levitical sacrifices, but we should continually thank and praise Him for the sacrifice He made for us. Instead of period- ically killing a lamb or a bullock, we periodically thank Him for allowing Himself to be killed for us. Instead of an annual pilgrimage to Jerusalem to offer sacrifice for our sins, we can daily make a pilgrimage to our prayer closets and thank God for taking our sins upon Himself and paying for them once and for all. Jesus paid the price in full—one time! We should continually, daily, constantly, and consistently thank our Lord Jesus Christ for sacrificing for us.

Show and Tell That There Are Many Ways to Say Thank You

What do cakes and wafers have anything to do with thanking God?

> If he offer it for a thanksgiving, then he shall offer with the sacrifice of thanksgiving unleavened cakes mingled with oil, and unleavened wafers anointed with oil, and cakes mingled with oil, of fine flour, fried. (Leviticus 7:12)

Yesterday's Israelites offered some wonderfully smelling cakes of bread fried in oil as a sacrifice of thanksgiving. (There's nothing like the aroma of fresh bread baking in the oven.) Today's Christians should show their thankful hearts to God by confessing His goodness (which is represented by His name) through verbal praise and obedient living. Just think about it. There are a number of lists that God has given us in Scripture that spell out some very specific ways that we can express our love to God through obedience. Those who know you are a believer will keep an eye on you to see if you practice what you preach. In other words, they will listen to your talk, watch your walk, and see if you balk when you are face-to-face with temptation. Here is a short list of some of God's lists.

- **The Ten Commandments**—ten ways to thank God for what He has done for you (Exodus 20:1–17).

- **The Fruits of the Spirit**—nine ways to show others your thankful, Spirit-controlled heart for God (Galatians 5:22–23).

- **The Beatitudes**—nine ways to express a thankful attitude to God (Matthew 5:1–12).

- **The Works of the Flesh**—seventeen ways to show God an "unthankful" heart and let Him know that you are in control and that He means nothing to you (Galatians 5:19–21).

- **The Great Commandment**—two ways to show God your thankful and loving heart (Mark 12:30–31).

For instance, how can Ten Commandments encourage a heart of thanksgiving? If you truly love God you will not take His name in vain but will praise His name; you will not put any other gods before Him but will thank Him for being the ever-loving, all-powerful God that He is; and you will set aside a special day to worship, honor, and thank Him for all He has done for you.

If you truly love others with all your heart, soul, and mind—intelligent, purposeful, committed love—you will thank God for those He has brought into your life, and you will not lie to them, you will not steal from them, you will not dishonor them, you will not get involved with immorality, you will not covet what they have, you will not kill them!

Every act of obedience to God's Word is a wonderful way to thank God for all He has done for you.

THE LAW OF CONSISTENCY

DANIEL 6:10

... as he did aforetime.

Show and Tell with Your Life the Kind of Consistency That Pleases God

Daniel went to his house and prayed, as he had consistently done for many years. Consistency sees each commitment as a special task from God and will sacrifice to accomplish the task regardless of the opposition. A consistent leader will have a steadfast reliability that can everyone can count on.

Daniel was a consistent leader. What he did aforetime, he did in the present time, and he scheduled it for a future time. He did not allow himself to be driven off course by the weather, health, weariness, or even a den of lions. He was consistent.

Show and Tell That Consistency Will Strengthen You When You Feel Like Quitting

Have you ever felt like you can't take it any longer, or that all you do is work, struggle, and agonize, but never win? When was the last time you felt like saying "I quit"? You are not alone. Many of us have felt the same way. Even those you think never struggle have had their times of discouragement.

The consistency of a good fighter or a good runner is not determined by how many fights they have won or how many races they have medaled in, but that they continued to fight when they were weary and continued to run even when they felt like quitting.

Even Paul did not look like a winner in the eyes of many of his peers. Remember, it did not say that he *won* the race, but that he *ran* the race.

> I have fought a good fight, I have finished my course, I have kept the faith. (2 Timothy 4:7)

It didn't say that he *won* the fight, but *fought* the fight. Second Timothy 4:7 people can never be accused of inconsistency. Paul was saying that he agonizingly fought through life and fulfilled God's revealed purpose for his life, and all the while he kept and guarded his personal trust in God through His Word.

Those things in our lives that we have no control over seem to be the most consistent. (These are the ones in which only God has the ultimate control.) I am thinking of beating hearts and breathing lungs. It is when you take control that you often lose consistency. For instance, you should ask yourself how consistent your prayer life is? How consistent are you in your devotional life? Are you experiencing consistent victory in your battle with the flesh? Do you have a consistent walk with God? Which heart beats the most consistently, your physical heart or your spiritual heart?

If you look closely, consistency can be seen in three words found in Paul's testimony in 2 Timothy 4:7—*fought, finished,* and *kept.* The Greek word for *fought* is *agōnizomai,* where we get our word agonize. And the word *fought* has the idea of contending, fighting, or wrestling for a victory. One writer said that the word meant to take pains, to wrestle, or to strain every nerve to the uttermost toward the goal. The synonyms also help us realize what Paul went through to be consistent. When Paul said he fought, he was implying that he struggled and toiled even to the point of feeling fatigue. Consistency does not come too easy. It is a fight.

The word *finished* (*teleō*) has the idea of accomplishing or completing something—not merely to stop or end it. It has the idea of bringing to perfection or reaching the destined goal. It not only completes the task, but completes it completely. We usually want to give up, or we get too tired to totally finish the task God has called us to do. For me, it is the task of growing in my own character the essential virtue of consistency. I cannot quit until I reach this goal.

While studying these three words, you can almost see Paul digging into a bag and pulling out something to illustrate each word. When he mentions "I have fought a good fight," I can see him pulling out boxing gloves and strapping them on. When he talks about "finishing the course," I can imagine him pulling out some Nike running shoes. For the phrase "kept the faith," he would probably pull out a military helmet, binoculars and a rifle. The word *kept* was used for wardens or guards who carefully kept watch from a guard tower.

So if I want to be a winner and not a loser in this war of consistency, I must do what Paul did. I must keep fighting even if it hurts, keep running even if I get completely weary, and keep trusting and believing what I have learned about my wonderful Lord and His Word.

Show and Tell That Consistency Can Be Seen at Every Sunrise and Every Sunset

When was the last time you woke early just to see a sunrise? I know we can Google it and see it online, but it is not the same. Not only will you be amazed how God makes orange and purple go together, just the fact that God does that every morning, day after day, without delay, is amazing.

> The sun also ariseth, and the sun goeth down, and hasteth to his place where he arose. (Ecclesiastes 1:5)

The consistency of the sun is not only incredible, it is mindboggling. Since the beginning of recorded history, the sun faithfully and consistently gets up every morning, gives us the light and warmth we need, and then heads to bed when its work is done. It takes a powerful Creator to create such consistency in our solar system. At whatever point the sun would oversleep or rebel against its Creator, we would either burn to a crisp or freeze to death.

Our God is a consistent God. A simple look at the rising and setting of the sun, the tracking of our solar system, or the thought of an ocean that is constantly being filled but never overflows, and you know we have a God who consistently holds our world together.

The more I think about how immutable and consistent God is, the more I am convicted about the inconsistencies in my own life.

You cannot hide your inconsistencies from your consistent God. You can hide them from each other and you can ignore them to yourselves, but God sees not only the inconsistency of your actions, but the inconsistencies of the motives behind your actions. Even though you may be consistent in your service, God knows whether such service was motivated by pleasing God, pleasing others, or pleasing self.

Whenever you try to play the consistency card, you lose. You attack someone for their inconsistency in an entertainment choice only to check your own viewing schedule for the past week and see the same inconsistencies. You question someone wasting two hours on a movie or a video game the same week you spent four hours on Monday Night Football. For every consistency you seem to pull off in a day, there are a dozen inconsistencies hidden in the same day planner.

It seems like you are blinded to the severity of your own inconsistencies, but almost have a supernatural x-ray vision to see the inconsistencies in others.

Romans 12:11 can help us. It says, "not slothful in business; fervent in spirit; serving the Lord." You can be consistent and lazy at the same time—consistently lazy. As a *sloth*, your consistent laziness will get you nowhere, and you'll accomplish nothing for God. The Lazy Daisies of our world feel entitled to everything but don't want to work for anything. They love handouts but refuse to get their hands dirty. In a way, I feel sorry for them. Even though they may have what others have because it was given to them disguised as their welfare, they never experience the joy of working for something and the feeling of accomplishment when they have sacrificed and saved to get what they wanted.

You cannot be consistently lazy and consistently fervent at the same time. Fervency in spirit is seen more in your passion, desire, and heart motivation than in what you have accomplished. It is like water that is boiling, even bubbling, and the steam caused by the heat is rattling the lid just waiting for a chance to boil over the side of the pot. It can't wait to get out and change the temperature around it. It doesn't like being held back and kept under lid. It wants to make a difference.

A servant who lacks consistency cannot be considered a true, biblical servant. If he lacks initiative (inconsistent in looking to see what needs to be done), if he lacks punctuality (inconsistent in getting to work on time or getting his projects done on time), if he lacks dependability (inconsistent in fulfilling what he consented to do), or if he lacks endurance (inconsistent in finishing a job well) he is not a true servant, but just someone working for a paycheck or serving to gain some personal worth or status. A true servant seeks to make his master successful and would never let inconsistencies distract him from his mission.

THE LAW OF REJECTION

DANIEL 6:II–I3

Then these men assembled, and found Daniel praying and making supplication before his God. Then they came near, and spake before the king concerning the king's decree; Hast thou not signed a decree, that every man that shall ask a petition of any God or man within thirty days, save of thee, O king, shall be cast into the den of lions? The king answered and said, The thing is true, according to the law of the Medes and Persians, which altereth not. Then answered they and said before the king, That Daniel, which is of the children of the captivity of Judah, regardeth not thee, O king, nor the decree that thou hast signed, but maketh his petition three times a day.

Show and Tell That a Life of Rejection Accompanies a Life that Pleases God

To think that someone doesn't like you is one thing, but to know that you are hated is quite another. The fear of rejection is a morbid fear. The feelings of rejection are miserable feelings, but the fact of rejection is a reality in every godly leader's life.

"*That* Daniel. You know, *that* slave from Judah. He ignores you. He pays no attention to you. He prays to *his* God three times a day. What a fool! Kill him. His kind—so high and mighty, thinking he is better than the rest of us—is not fit to live. Let the lions tear him from limb to limb! We hate him, and you have to kill him. Today!"

As a lion-like leader committed to the ministry of reconciliation (helping others draw closer to the Lord) you will face many who will assume that you look down on them or that you are judging them just because you sense their need of spiritual help. There are those who will resist you, and therefore reject you, because they think they are already as close to God as anyone else they know. There are those who will disagree with your definition of "being close to God" and will reject both your counsel and you. Then there are those who don't want to be close to God, and being close to you, as you seek to stay close to God, forces them to reject you.

Rejection knows what it means to be deliberately excluded, actively bullied, or passively ignored.

The reasons for rejection are varied. Some are excluded because they are different—different in looks, dress, or beliefs. Some are bullied because they are viewed as inferior. Some are ignored because they are a threat. Some are snubbed because their godliness makes the ungodly uncomfortable.

Godly leaders are different than the norm; godly leaders set a higher standard of living; godly leaders are a threat to the prevalent sinful and selfish attitude of mediocrity; godly leaders make the ungodly uncomfortable; godly leaders will be rejected. Just like Daniel and just like our Lord Jesus Christ, so you will be rejected if you strive to be a godly leader.

> Yea, and all that will live godly in Christ Jesus shall suffer persecution. (2 Timothy 3:12)

Show and Tell that Hate and Rejection Were No Strangers to Our Lord

ISAIAH 1:2-4

Hear, O heavens, and give ear, O earth; for the Lord has spoken: "Children have I reared and brought up, but they have rebelled against me. The ox knows its owner, and the donkey its master's crib, but Israel does not know, my people do not understand." Ah, sinful nation, a people laden with iniquity,

offspring of evildoers, children who deal corruptly! They
have forsaken the Lord, they have despised the Holy One of
Israel, they are utterly estranged. (ESV)

JOHN 1:11

He came unto His own, and His own received Him not.

To illustrate Isaiah 1:2–4 and John 1:11, let's join in on a
fictitious (but very possible) conversation between a pastor
and some from his college class from church.

Pastor Andy walks into the *Ugly Mug*, a popular down-
town coffee shop, and sees nine college students from his
church sipping lattes and looking extremely serious in their
discussion. As he approaches their table, Lindsey, Katie, Abi,
Meghan, Ethan, Kyle, Cara, Shellie, and Kristine all look up,
look at each other, and then smile.

Abi: (the spokesperson of the group) Pastor Andy, we
were just talking about you! We were going to
ask you tomorrow at church if you had time to
answer a hard question for us. But since you are
here, do you have some time? Like 100 hours?

Pastor: Sure. Let me get my coffee and I'll join you.

Cara: I'll get it for you, what do you like?

Pastor: Ah, I normally get decaf with skim milk and
Sweet'n Low.

Cara: I think they call that a Why Bother.

(all laugh)

Pastor: OK, so what is your big question?

Kyle: We are wondering why the world seems to
be so hateful towards Christ and committed
Christians. At college, we try to be nice, helpful,
tolerant, and still once they know we won't party
with them or hang with them they get vicious.

Shellie: The bottom line is, we hate being hated!

Pastor: I understand. It seems like the more love we offer the more hate we receive. Well, first of all, you are in great company. Do any of you have a Bible with you? Look up John 7:5 and 12:37 and read it for us.

Ethan: I've got John 7:5. "For neither did His brethren believe in Him."

Katie: I have John 12:37. "But though He had done so many miracles before them, yet they believed not on Him."

Pastor: Jesus was who He said He was. He was God in the flesh, living a perfectly sinless life. Such goodness embarrasses those who are selfish. Such goodness is a threat to their self-image and their acceptance by others. Many reject those who are not just like them, therefore Jesus is bound to be rejected because as the Holy One of God, He will never be *just like* selfish, sinful men.

I too have wrestled with this and memorized a series of Bible phrases that helped. Let's see if I can still remember them.
"Marvel not, my brethren, if the world hate you."
"If the world hate you, ye know that it hated me before it hated you."
"And ye shall be hated of all men for my name's sake: but he that endureth to the end shall be saved."
"Blessed are ye, when men shall revile you, and persecute you, and shall say all manner of evil against you falsely, for my sake."
"Blessed are ye, when men shall hate you, and when they shall separate you from their company, and shall reproach you, and cast out your name as evil, for the Son of man's sake."
I think the references are 1 John 3:13, John 15:18, Matthew 10:22, Matthew 5:11, and Luke

6:22. You can see God has much to say about being rejected and hated for His sake.

Meghan: Hate is a harsh word. Hate hurts! I think that hearts filled with hate often do not think rationally, cannot be reasoned with, and end up saying and doing things that are only regretted later. Hate is hurtful to both the hated and the hater.

Abi: Hate hates to be confronted. Hate hates to be proved wrong. Hate is everything that God is not.

Kyle: I heard someone say that your identification with Christ immediately supplies you with a bullseye for the hateful to see.

Pastor: If believers hated Satan and his evil as much as unbelievers hate Jesus Christ, we would see a revival in our hearts and churches of unsurpassed proportion.

Lindsey: Christ said to, "Marvel not . . . if the world hate you." I try not to marvel, but I do have a hard time understanding *why* the world hates Jesus Christ so. What has He done to make them so angry? He created them. He loves them. He offers forgiveness to them. He died for them to bring them to God. Why is the world so upset? It is men who are hurtful, abusive, and wicked, not God. The world hates war—so does God. The world hates abuse—so does God. The world hates even the thought of hell—so does God! Why is the world so angry and hateful towards God? A huge portion of our world's population are taught and trained that if someone accepts Christ and Christianity, they should be killed. Why? I guess we should ask Satan instead of God. He started this whole hate movement. I may be wrong, but I think that he thinks he is going to win in the end. He won't. Those who have chosen to be deceived by Satan and those who have accepted his lies as truth will someday realize their foolishness when they kneel before the God of truth. Then the hate that Satan has immersed the world in will be turned on him by the thousands and millions that will be separated from God for eternity.

Kristine: So Nicodemus comes to Christ asking some great questions. He, as a religious leader, sees the hate movement towards Jesus but cannot join in. He may have been wondering the same thing we are, "Why do so many hate this Jesus of Nazareth?" Before Jesus explains why He is hated so, He makes sure that His love, redemption, and offer of eternal life are available to everyone that hates Him. It is hard not to *marvel* at the world's hateful rejection of such a free gift of grace. Here is a portion of what Jesus shared with Nicodemus in John 3, "For God so loved the world that He gave His only begotten Son, that whoever believes in Him should not perish but have everlasting life. For God did not send His Son into the world to condemn the world, but that the world through Him might be saved. He who believes in Him is not condemned; but he who does not believe is condemned already, because he has not believed in the name of the only begotten Son of God. And this is the condemnation, that the light has come into the world, and men loved darkness rather than light, because their deeds were evil. For everyone practicing evil hates the light and does not come to the light, lest his deeds should be exposed. But he who does the truth comes to the light, that his deeds may be clearly seen, that they have been done in God."

Pastor: Wow. I can see you guys have done some serious thinking about all of this. Your willingness to deal with this and to be hated for the cause of

Christ does my heart as a pastor so much good. You know, I can't completely answer your question why Christ and Christians are hated so, but we can do what Peter and the other apostles did when they were not only hated, but beaten for teaching about Jesus Christ. Shellie, read Acts 5:40-42 for us.

Shellie: "And they agreed with him, and when they had called for the apostles and beaten them, they commanded that they should not speak in the name of Jesus, and let them go. So they departed from the presence of the council, rejoicing that they were counted worthy to suffer shame for His name. And daily in the temple, and in every house, they did not cease teaching and preaching Jesus as the Christ."

Pastor: If we can do the same, and rejoice that we are even counted worthy to suffer for our Lord, God will be so pleased. Thanks for inviting me to your table. We've been so engrossed in our conversation, I forgot to drink my coffee.

All: Why bother?

NUMBER TWELVE

THE LAW OF INNOCENCE

DANIEL 6:21-23

Then said Daniel unto the king, O king, live forever. My God hath sent his angel, and hath shut the lions' mouths, that they have not hurt me: forasmuch as **before him innocency was found in me**; and also before thee, O king, have I done no hurt. Then was the king exceeding glad for him, and commanded that they should take Daniel up out of the den. So Daniel was taken up out of the den, and no manner of hurt was found upon him, because he believed in his God.

Show and Tell with Your Life the Kind of Innocence That Pleases God

There is nothing that appeases the conscience more than a clear conscience. Sin not, and you will not suffer the consequences of sin. Sin not, and you'll never fear being caught in your sin. No one really loses their innocence, they usually give it away. To enjoy the innocence of a child in our teen and adult years, we must become childlike, but not childish. Innocence has a peaceful blamelessness about it. When you know you have done nothing wrong, you can be at perfect peace with God and others.

Innocence has no defensive bones in its entire body. Innocence knows no shades of gray. It is black and white. Either you are innocent or you are not! Innocence is not a result of blameshifting or excuse making. You may cover up your actions, but that does not make you innocent.

Innocence breeds confidence! Daniel could confidently say, "innocency was found in me." He knew his heart; he knew his motives; and he knew he had done nothing wrong.

Innocence smiles when attacked or accused, knowing that somehow, someway, someday the truth will prevail.

Show and Tell That True Innocence Is Dependent on God's Protective Hand

If you have ever played high school football or spent some time in the quarterback's position, you remember feeling like you had only seconds from the time the ball was hiked before three freight trains collided with you in the middle of the crash. It is hard to measure the intensity that motivates a massive lineman to keep a 285-pound tackle from sacking the quarterback. Because we often lack the spiritual intensity needed to stay pure, we need the powerful staying hand of God to keep us from sacking ourselves.

> Keep back thy servant also from presumptuous [or deliberate] sins; let them not have dominion over me [dominate me or control my life]: then shall I be upright [which means blameless or free of guilt], and I shall be innocent from the great transgression. Let the words of my mouth [spoken words], and the meditation of my heart [unspoken thoughts], be acceptable in thy sight, O Lord, my strength, and my redeemer. (Psalm 19:13–14.)

I have often prayed David's prayer, "Lord, hold me back from life-dominating, premeditative sin." We cannot expect to be innocent and continue in our sin, whether it is fear, worry, anger, or lust. Our hearts are so depraved at times that we act like vicious guard dogs heavily chained to iron posts who jerk their heads back every time they race toward would-be victims. We need God's hand on our leash each time our sinful flesh wants to take control.

True innocence is a result of God's protective hand, protecting us from ourselves. Remember Daniel? God kept the lions' mouths shut because he was innocent before God. How innocent are you?

Show and Tell That Jesus Lived an Innocent Life while on Earth and Continues to Be Innocent of Any Accusations Thrown His Way by Troubled Men

Judas Iscariot recognized Jesus' innocence when he said, "I have sinned in that I have betrayed the innocent blood" (Matthew 27:4) Remember, Jesus died for your sin and my sin. He was sinless. He was innocent.

Have you ever been accused of lying when you know before God that you didn't? For whatever reason, your friends took your accusers side by believing them and not you. Truth always prevails in time. Your accusers will be embarrassed when they realize that you did not lie and will hopefully make it right with you. By the way, you are in good company. Did you know that Judas, the apostle that betrayed Jesus, lied about the innocence of Jesus? And his lie killed himself and Jesus. We, like Christ, may suffer for something that we have not done, but that does not mean we are not innocent, blameless, and free from guilt of what we are accused of.

- Judas finally recognized Jesus' innocence: "I have betrayed the innocent blood." (Matthew 27:4)

- The dying thief recognized the innocence of Christ: "This man hath done nothing amiss." (Luke 23:41)

- Pilate's wife knew of Jesus' innocence: "Have thou nothing to do with that just man." (Matthew 27:19)

- Pilate knew Jesus was innocent: "I am innocent of the blood of this just person." (Matthew 27:24)

- Peter knew of Christ's innocence: "Christ, as of a lamb without blemish and without spot." (1 Peter 1:19)

And now we are reminded that Jesus was the sinless Son of God; He lived an innocent life, and still does! We had better recognize the innocency of our Lord and never accuse Him of not caring, not loving, or not wanting our best.

Show and Tell That Jesus' Innocence and Blamelessness Is the Key to Our Own Innocence and Blamelessness Before Him

We know that Jesus was innocent because He never sinned. But we also know our own hearts and know that they are far from innocent. Is there any way we can even hope to be innocent before God someday?

Jesus was just *just*! To be *just* is to be innocent. To be blameless is to be innocent. To be free from guilt is to be innocent.

> When Pilate saw that he could prevail nothing, but that rather a tumult was made, he took water, and washed his hands before the multitude, saying, I am innocent of the blood of this just person: see ye to it. (Matthew 27:24)

Pilate washed his hands of the whole situation. He symbolically made a statement that he was not attacking the innocency of Jesus of Nazareth. What he did not know was that his statement, "I am innocent of the blood of this just person" was not true. None of us are innocent, because we are all sinners. Peter put it so well, "For Christ also hath once suffered for sins [not His sins, but my sins], the just for the unjust [the innocent for the guilty, the blameless for the blamable, the guiltless for the guilty], that He might bring us to God!" (1 Peter 3:18)

There is a common message woven through some colorful passages of Scripture that hint towards blamelessness and innocency. What was true with the sacrificial lamb, was true with the Lamb of God; what is true with the Lamb of God, should be the goal for every believer. This is the knowledge that only through God's grace, mercy, and forgiveness can we see our blemishes vanish and spots disappear. As the living Word uses the written Word, our hearts are cleansed from all unrighteousness.

> Speak ye unto all the congregation of Israel, saying, In the tenth day of this month they shall take to them every man a lamb, according to the house of their fathers, a lamb for an house: and if the household be too little for the lamb, let him and his neighbor next unto his house take it according to the number of the souls; every man according to his eating shall make your count for the lamb. **Your lamb shall be without blemish,** a male of the first year: ye shall take it out from the sheep, or from the goats. (Exodus 12:3–5)

> All we like sheep have gone astray; we have turned every one to his own way; and the Lord hath laid on Him the iniquity of us all. He was oppressed, and He was afflicted, yet He opened not His mouth: **He is brought as a lamb to the slaughter**, and as a sheep before her shearers is dumb, so He openeth not His mouth. (Isaiah 53:6–7)

> Forasmuch as ye know that ye were not redeemed with corruptible things, as silver and gold, from your vain conversation received by tradition from your fathers; but with the precious blood of Christ, as of a lamb **without blemish and without spot**. (1 Peter 1:18–19)

> Wherefore, beloved, seeing that ye look for such things, be diligent that ye may be found of Him in peace, **without spot, and blameless**. (2 Peter 3:14)

> Husbands, love your wives, even as Christ also loved the church, and gave himself for it; that he might sanctify and cleanse it with the washing of water by the word, that he might present it to himself a glorious church, **not having**

spot, or wrinkle, or any such thing; but that it should be holy and without blemish. (Ephesians 5:25–27)

And the very God of peace sanctify you wholly; and I pray God your whole spirit and soul and body **be preserved blameless** unto the coming of our Lord Jesus Christ. Faithful is He that calleth you, who also will do it. (1 Thessalonians 5:23–24)

Our innocence is God's desire. Let me finish our list of verses with Philippians 2:13–16.

For it is God which worketh in you both to will and to do of His good pleasure. Do all things without murmurings and disputings: that ye may be **blameless and harmless**, the sons of God, without rebuke, in the midst of a crooked and perverse nation, among whom ye shine as lights in the world; holding forth the word of life; that I may rejoice in the day of Christ, that I have not run in vain, neither labored in vain.

God will do what He wills in our lives, if we cooperate with Him.

THE LAW OF FAITH
————•————

DANIEL 6:23

Then was the king exceedingly glad for him, and commanded that they should take Daniel up out of the den. So Daniel was taken up out of the den, and no manner of hurt was found upon him, be-cause he believed in his God.

Show and Tell with Your Life the Kind of Faith That Pleases God

Daniel believed in his God "who through faith . . . stopped the mouths of lions" (Hebrews 11:33).

Now faith is the substance of things hoped for [confident expectation], the evidence of things not seen. (Hebrews 11:1)

But without faith it is impossible to please him: for he that cometh to God must believe that he is, and that he is a re-warder of them that diligently seek him. (Hebrews 11:6)

Faith simply trusts God to do what He promises to do; faith is assured that God is sovereign and knows what is best; faith is confident that God is almighty with the power to do whatever He desires.

I never struggle with having the faith to believe that God can do anything; I struggle in knowing whether He wills to do what I want Him to do. Use what little faith you have and watch God increase it. Our love for God (because of what He has done for us) motivates us to take those first baby steps of faith. As we grow in love, we learn to walk by faith; if we continue to grow, our walking matures to the point of being able "to run and not be weary."

The more time we spend with God the better we know God.

> So then faith cometh by hearing, and hearing by the word of God. (Romans 10:17)

The better we know God the more we love God. The more we love God the more time we want to spend with God. Et cetera. Et cetera. Et cetera.

Show and Tell That Little Faith Can Grow into Much Faith

> And the apostles said unto the Lord, Increase our faith. (Luke 17:5)

The story that Jesus shared about the Apostles struggling with faith is a story told over and over again. As a young leader, you may still struggle with having the faith to forgive those who have sinned against you. In the dialog below, replace "Kate" with your name or someone you know.

Kate: Mom why? Why did dad leave us? We don't have any money. Doesn't he care? We can hardly afford our rent. I don't want to hate him, but I really don't know how I can ever forgive him.

Mom: Kate, you know your dad does not know the Lord and is really struggling right now. Every time he hurts you by his yelling and cursing, he always comes back and asks you to forgive him.

Kate: Yeah, but how do I know he means it? How many times do I have to forgive him?

Kate is not the first to ask that question. We all have wrestled with this issue way too many times. It is one of those things that God will do through us if we let Him. The twelve disciples asked the same question in Luke 17:1–6.

> Then said he unto the disciples, It is impossible but that offences will come: but woe unto him, through whom they come! It were better for him that a millstone were hanged about his neck, and he cast into the sea, than that he should offend one of these little ones. Take heed to yourselves: If thy brother trespass against thee, rebuke him; and if he repent, forgive him. And if he trespass against thee seven times in a day, and seven times in a day turn again to thee, saying, I repent; thou shalt forgive him. And the apostles said unto the Lord, Increase our faith. And the Lord said, If ye had faith as a grain of mustard seed, ye might say unto this sycamine tree, Be thou plucked up by the root, and be thou planted in the sea; and it should obey you.

We may not be asked to forgive seven times a day, but certainly seven times a month is not uncommon. In response to the Lord's teaching on forgiving the same guy over and over again, these rough fishermen turned preachers said, "Lord, increase our faith!" Believing that such spiritual strength to forgive would be given them when they prayed was a stretch for these apostles.

The Lord in a way was saying, "Use what little faith you have, and I promise I'll give you more."

Commentator John Butler has some wonderful thoughts on this in his book entitled, *The Analytical Bible Expositor.*

Butler quotes Luke 17:5 "Increase our faith" in the section titled "The Enthusiasm about Faith." And then he says, "This is such a noble request. It shows the enthusiasm the disciples had for faith. They did not ask Christ to increase their finances or their fame or their fun, but they asked Him to increase their faith. This is not a popular request among Christians, for they have so little enthusiasm for faith. They would much prefer an increase in their finances and fame and fun."[1]

The second section is entitled "The Encouragement for Faith." "If ye had faith as a grain of mustard seed, ye might say unto this sycamine tree, Be thou plucked up by the root, and be thou planted in the sea; and it should obey you" (Luke 17:6). Christ would encourage the disciples' faith by showing them that just a little faith—symbolized here by the mustard seed which was used as a symbol of extreme smallness—would accomplish wonders. The extent of the accomplishment here is in the emphasis on the roots. Sycamine trees were known for an extensive root system so to uproot it was an extra special achievement."[2]

The third point starts with, "The Enlargement of Faith." "If ye had faith as a grain of mustard seed . . ." (Luke 17:6). Christ responded to the request to have the disciples' faith enlarged by encouraging them to use what faith they had. Using what faith we have will help to enlarge our faith; just as using what muscles we have is the way to have stronger muscles. The disciples doubtless wanted some magical formula that would give them great faith. Christ gave them a formula, but it was not a glamorous gift but an exhortation to use what they had, and this would give them more faith."[3]

In very much the same way, Elijah encouraged the starving widow of Zarephath to use what little faith (and food) she had and watch God take care of her and give her more faith (and food).

> Then the word of the Lord came to him, saying, "Arise, go to Zarephath, which belongs to Sidon, and dwell there. See, I have commanded a widow there to provide for you." So he arose and went to Zarephath. And when he came to the gate of the city, indeed a widow was there gathering sticks. And he called to her and said, "Please bring me a little water in a cup, that I may drink." And as she was going to get it, he called to her and said, "Please bring me a morsel of bread in your hand."
>
> So she said, "As the Lord your God lives, I do not have bread, only a handful of flour in a bin, and a little oil in a jar; and

see, I am gathering a couple of sticks that I may go in and prepare it for myself and my son, that we may eat it, and die."

And Elijah said to her, "Do not fear; go and do as you have said, but make me a small cake from it first, and bring it to me; and afterward make some for yourself and your son. For thus says the Lord God of Israel: 'The bin of flour shall not be used up, nor shall the jar of oil run dry, until the day the Lord sends rain on the earth.' "

So she went away and did according to the word of Elijah; and she and he and her household ate for many days. The bin of flour was not used up, nor did the jar of oil run dry, according to the word of the Lord which He spoke by Elijah."
(1 Kings 17:8–16 NKJV)

Although Kate may feel that she could never have enough faith to forgive her dad, God promises to give her more faith if she would exercise the faith He has already given her. God will do the same for all who desire the faith to forgive. Even you!

Show and Tell That the Lord Knows How Much Faith We Have, How Much We Need, and How Much He Will Graciously Give to Us

Cancer. Alzheimer's. Stroke. Heart attack. A broken relationship. Loss of a job. Death of a loved one.

Do you ever wonder why God just doesn't completely heal those we love? Do you blame yourself for not having enough faith? We all have wrestled with all kinds of emotions and feelings through life's journey. God will teach us that it is not the amount of faith, but the object of our faith that counts. I have often prayed, "Lord, I know you can, but I don't know if you will!" I never struggle with having the faith to believe that God can do anything; I struggle in knowing whether He wills to do what I want Him to do.

Jesus said unto him, If thou canst believe, all things are possible to him that believeth. And straightway the father of the child cried out, and said with tears, Lord, I believe; help Thou mine unbelief. (Mark 9:23–24)

God *could* get rid of all the cancer in the world. He *could* stop all heart disease and accidents. But in a way, it is not cancer or heart disease that kills. God has a specific time when He wants us to come into this world and has a set time when He wants all believers to go on to heaven. It could be an accident, a heart attack, a prolonged illness, or cancer. God will answer our prayers and completely heal all someday. You ask "When?" It looks like for many, God is going to wait until He takes them to heaven. Because there in heaven, their cancer, their heart issues, and their Alzheimer's will be no more. All of us are dying, some just faster than others.

Show and Tell That Faith Grows As We Use What We Have and Watch God Supply the Rest

Paul, Silas, and Timothy thanked God and bragged to others about how much the young believers in Thessalonica grew in faith. Could the same be said for you or your family this past year?

> We are bound [obliged or impelled] to thank God always for you, brethren, as it is meet, because that **your faith groweth exceedingly**, and the **charity** [love] of every one of you all toward each other **aboundeth**; so that we ourselves glory in you in the churches of God for your patience and faith in all your persecutions and tribulations that ye endure. (2 Thessalonians 1:3–4)

Sometimes it is not easy to objectively measure faith. Although you cannot weigh it or get a tape measure around it, you can see it grow in very specific ways. Paul saw the growing faith of the Thessalonians in two ways.

1. Love—they abundantly loved each other.

2. Patience—they patiently endured difficult persecutions and tribulations.

Why is it such a joy to be commended for these two diamond-quality characteristics? They both reveal a proper life focus. Selfishness focuses on me, my needs, my time, my money, my comfort, my life, me! True love keeps its focus on those loved and not on self. Genuine patience keeps its focus on God's wisdom and sovereignty and accepts difficult situations without giving God deadlines to remove them. In essence, these young Thessalonians were simply fulfilling what Christ emphasized in His response to a crooked lawyer's attempt to trip Him up in Matthew 22:37–39. "You shall love the Lord your God with all your heart, with all your soul, with all your mind" and also, "you shall love your neighbor as yourself."

Could the same be said for you and your family this past year?

NUMBER FOURTEEN

THE LAW OF INFLUENCE

DANIEL 6:25–28

Then king Darius wrote unto all people, nations, and languages, that dwell in all the earth; peace be multiplied unto you. I make a decree, That in every dominion of my kingdom men tremble and fear before the God of Daniel: For he is the living God, and steadfast forever, and his kingdom [is the one that] shall not be destroyed, and his dominion shall [endure] to the end. He delivereth and rescueth, And he worketh signs and wonders in heaven and in earth, who hath delivered Daniel from the power of the lions. So this Daniel prospered in the reign of Darius and in the reign of Cyrus the Persian.

Show and Tell with Your Life the Kind of Influence That Pleases God

Daniel refused to be affected by the cultural influences he was forced to live in. He knew what it meant to be *in* the world but not *of* the world. Instead of being influenced by those around him, he chose to be influenced by God.

Daniel made a difference in the life of King Darius, in the reign of King Cyrus, in the lives of many Babylonians. Influence is impacting individuals. Spiritual influence is impacting individuals for eternity. Influence is making a difference in lives for their good and God's glory. Influence always focuses on the betterment of others rather than the exaltation of self. Although influence is to sway, to compel, or to persuade, it can impact others for evil as much as for good. Some are easily influenced and others are rarely influenced.

Surround yourself with good influences and you'll be influenced for good. Thermometers are easily influenced by thermostats. We have to choose which we want to be.

- Who controls the spiritual temperature in your life?
- Who have you influenced in the past year?
- Who is closer to the Lord today because of your influence yesterday?
- Whose life will never be the same because they spent time with you?
- Whose influence has God used to impact your life?
- Whose godly influence has swayed, impressed, or persuaded you to change something in your life?

The more we allow ourselves to be influenced by God through His Word and Spirit, the more we will be able to influence others for good and godliness.

Show and Tell That Influence Can Be Passed Down from Generation to Generation

Now the God of hope fill you with all joy and peace in believing, that ye may abound in hope, through the power of the Holy Ghost. And I myself also am persuaded of you, my brethren, that ye also are full of goodness, filled with all knowledge, able also to admonish one another. (Romans 15:13–14)

Can you imagine the following scenario happening today? This fictitious situation can happen, has happened, and hopefully will happen again. Concentrate on how this guy named Perry followed the teaching of Romans 15:13–14. How could you do the same?

Josh: Hey guys, would you guys mind going out for a steak after work on Friday night? We have to get this last section framed in by the weekend, which means some late nights this week, but I have something I'd love to challenge you guys with. Friday night?

Caleb: Fine with us!

Mike: He is a great guy to work for. Not only is he helping us with our college school bill, but I love what he is teaching us about work and life.

Seth: Yeah, what do you think he wants to challenge us with?

Hank: Have you ever watched him with the junior high guys at church? He really is burdened for them. It would not surprise me if it had to do with some of those young guys.

Caleb: Well, we'll meet on Friday, and we will find out. So let's get back to work and get this roof framed.

(Friday at the Beef House)

Josh: These have got to be some of the best steaks I've ever seen. They melt in your mouth.

Caleb: Thanks so much for the treat. I'm stuffed.

Mike: And thanks also for giving us the work to help for college. I can't tell you how this takes pressure off during the year.

Josh: Well, you guys are definitely earning it. I've got a burden that I want to share with you guys. I have known you four brothers for a number of years and am pleased with your spiritual growth and desires. Now I want to challenge you to take it all a step further. We have a number of sixth, seventh, and eighth grade boys that need a spiritual shot in the arm and need to man-up regarding the things of God. I know God can use you guys in their lives. My mind goes to Romans 15:13–14 "Now the God of hope fill you

with all joy and peace in believing, that ye may
abound in hope, through the power of the Holy
Ghost. And I myself also am persuaded of you,
my brethren, that ye also are full of goodness,
filled with all knowledge, able also to admonish
one another."

God has filled or influenced your lives with His
joy, peace, goodness, and knowledge for a reason. So you can influence others. Paul used the
word *admonish*, which simply means it is time
for you guys to impact or influence these young
guys the way I've been able to help you through
the years.

Seth: Where would you want us to start?

Josh: Personal devotions and prayer life. If you each
pick two guys to encourage and check up on,
you guys could help them learn how to spend
time with God just like you do!

Hank: Do you have any certain boys in mind?

Josh: I do. I want you guys to connect with the eight
boys in my Sunday school class that already
have tender hearts for the Lord. These are the
ones that will make a difference in our youth
group and church in the future.

Caleb: Will you help us in this? Like if they ask a question that we don't know how to answer?

Josh: You know I will. Years ago, a faithful logger influenced my life for Christ, so I have spent some
time influencing you guys, so you can influence
these young boys, so someday they will influence others. I think this is the way God intended
it to work.

Show and Tell That Influence Can Be Sung to Others

Music has a major place in our lives. Many of you reading this book are incredibly gifted in music. God created music. God loves music. God sings about us! God gifts many individuals to use music to influence others. God uses music to influence lives for His glory.

> Let the word of Christ dwell in [influence] you richly in all wisdom; teaching and admonishing [influencing] one another in psalms and hymns and spiritual songs, singing with grace in your hearts to the Lord. (Colossians 3:16)

I have a challenge for you musicians. As the Word of Christ influences you, you can influence others through psalms, hymns, and spiritual songs as others hear you sing heartfelt songs of gracious thankfulness to the Lord. At whatever point you can influence others to be as thankful for their salvation as you are for yours, you are fulfilling the Colossians 3:16 challenge.

When you study the word *admonish* you will find that the Greek word, *noutheteo*, is translated *admonish*, *warn*, and *exhort*. If through our music we can warn our friends of unbiblical thinking and exhort them to walk with God, then we can know that we are using our gifts in music in a way that God intended.

Show and Tell that Influence Wears Many Hats

> Now we exhort [influence] you, brethren, warn [influence] them that are unruly, comfort [influence] the feebleminded, support [influence] the weak, be patient [influence] toward all men. (1 Thessalonians 5:14)

The **Exhortation Hat** looks much like a soft, golfer's hat. With this hat on, influence walks right up to an individual, stands by their side, and lets them know that he is there and ready to go through whatever trial they are facing. He will stand *with* them. He is there with his golfer's hat on to help, comfort, and encourage.

> As ye know how we exhorted and comforted and charged every one of you, as a father doth his children, that ye would walk worthy of God, who hath called you unto his kingdom and glory. (1 Thessalonians 2:11–12)

Influence's **Warning Hat** reminds me of a police hat— short bill, blue, with a look of authority. Each time influence puts on his police like warning hat, it goes to work doing what needs to be done even though it is not always fun to do so. Just like a warning light, a warning signal, or a warning label, influence reminds you that if you continue in the direction you are going, there will be harsh and severe consequences. An influential warning from a biblical perspective can deter us from making life choices that would be regretted for many years to come. The unruly straighten up when influence shows up with his warning hat on.

> I write not these things to shame you, but as my beloved sons I **warn** you. (1 Corinthians 4:14)

The **Comfort Hat** is one of influence's favorites. It is nothing more than a warm, woolen stocking hat that hugs your head on a cold winter day. It consoles, speaks kindly, soothingly comforts, and lessens the tension in every situation. The terrified, terror-stricken fainthearted usually stop their fretting and worrying when influence shows up with his warm stocking hat on. Just the sight of him lets them know everything is going to be OK.

> The Jews then which were with her in the house, and **comforted her**, when they saw Mary, that she rose up hastily and went out, followed her, saying, She goeth unto the grave to weep there. Then when Mary was come where Jesus was, and saw him, she fell down at his feet, saying unto him, Lord, if thou hadst been here, my brother had not died. When Jesus

therefore saw her weeping, and the Jews also weeping which
came with her, he groaned in the spirit, and was troubled,
and said, Where have ye laid him? They said unto Him,
Lord, come and see. Jesus wept. (John 11:31–35)

The **Support Hat** is the traditional hard hat seen at most
construction sights. Some are yellow, and some are white,
but when you see a hard hat in the area, you know there are
guys who know how to keep everything from crashing down.
Influence puts his hard hat on when those around him need
someone to hold on to when they are about to fall. Those
who are weak and lack strength to stand on their own, need
the comforting, supportive role of influence. Matthew 6:24
says, "No man can serve two masters: for either he will hate
the one, and love the other; or else he will **hold to** the one
(firmly hold on to, be loyal to), and despise the other. Ye
cannot serve God and mammon." Titus 1:9 says, "**Holding
fast** (tightly attaching yourself to) the faithful word as he hath
been taught, that he may be able by sound doctrine both to
exhort and to convince the gainsayers."

The **Patient Hat** is what influence wears most of the time.
It is nothing more than your ordinary, everyday well-worn
ball cap. When influence puts his everyday ball cap on, he
faces a normal day which involves accepting difficult people
and difficult situations as part of life and ministry. Although
some people are prickly and some problems are painful,
when influence puts his patience hat on he is not hasty or
quick to be frustrated or angry with anyone or any situation.
He accepts it from God. He refuses to say or do anything that
would hinder or even eliminate his influence in the lives of
those God has brought into his path. He lovingly waits for all
men—no favorites, no special interest groups, no teacher's
pets. He patiently waits in all situations—no manipulation,
no taking things into his own hands, no begging God to
get out of the difficulty but only requesting strength to get
through the trial. Influence has the patience to hang with the

unruly rebellious, the feebleminded worriers, and the fragile weak. Meditate on these phrases.

Love suffers long. (1 Corinthians 13:4 NKJV)

The Lord . . . is longsuffering toward us. (2 Peter 3:9 NKJV)

Be patient. Establish your hearts, for the coming of the Lord draws nigh [and is getting closer every day]. (James 5:8 NKJV)

Show and Tell That We Choose Who or What Influences Our Lives

A DUI on your record is not going to help your insurance premiums, your bank account, or your testimony. A DUI puts many lives in danger, including your own. In a way, God comments on DUIs. Actually He does. Ephesians 5:18 is God's way of describing a DUI.

And be not drunk with wine, wherein is excess; but be filled with the Spirit. (Ephesians 5:18)

Driving under the influence of alcohol is not only illegal; it is illogical, ill-advised, and plain old stupid. It doesn't make sense to purposely put yourself under some outside influence that could result in the loss of your license, or even worse, the loss of the life of a young mother and her two-year-old son that you *accidentally* hit head-on while driving in your semidrunken state. God says, "Be not drunk with wine." Hard liquors are evil slave masters. Their enslaving influence forces many to do what they would never do otherwise. A man who is drunk as a skunk causes a greater stink than any polecat. Drunken men are no strangers to cursing, lewdness, fighting, and even abuse of those they love. Those who are pulled over for a DUI may not only wreck their car, if they continue being influenced in such ways, they'll totally wreck their lives and many others.

So what does a DUI have to do with being "filled with the Spirit"?

One influences you for evil, and the other influences you for good. Both can and will influence the way you talk, the way you think, the way you reason, the way you fight temptation, the way you love yourself, and the way you love the Lord.

CONCLUSION

The influence the Holy Spirit can have on our lives is overwhelming. We should never forget the gospel message of Christ dying for us and willingly, but undeservedly, taking our sin's punishment on Himself. The wage or payment of sin is death—eternal death, eternal separation from God. None of us can accumulate enough good to get to God. We all fall short of God's glorious perfection. So Jesus, who lived a perfect life, died for us all, was buried, then rose again, and went back to heaven. Remember Jesus Christ is God in the flesh. He is the visible icon of the invisible God. When Jesus left this earth to return to heaven, He sent His Holy Spirit back to dwell or live in the hearts of those who trust Him and Him alone for the forgiveness of their sins. We all need Christ and the influence of His Holy Spirit in our lives.

Daniel lived with lion-like integrity and his life revealed the fourteen laws of courageous leadership we have just studied together. Daniel is with the Lord today enjoying life in the very presence of God.

You can keep courageous, lion-like leaders off the endangered species list and out of extinction. How?

- Become one.

- Recruit another.

We need more Daniels and Danielles in our world today. Daniel was a lion-like leader, and you can be too.

ENDNOTES

Introduction

1. "Are Lions Endangered?" *All About Wildlife*, accessed September 30, 2015, http://www.allaboutwildlife.com/endangered-species/are-lions-endangered/5825.

2. "NatureServe conservation status," accessed September 30, 2015, https://en.wikipedia.org/wiki/NatureServe_conservation_status#Numbers.

PART ONE—LIVING WITH LION-LIKE INTEGRITY

A Meditation on Daniel 6

1. E. M. Bounds, *Purpose in Prayer* (New York: Fleming H. Revell Company, 1920), 66.

2. http://www.crosswalk.com/faith/women/40-powerful-quotes-from-corrie-ten-boom.html.

3. *Spurgeon's Pulpit Sermons* (Seattle: Biblesoft, Inc., 2006).

PART TWO—GUARDING AGAINST EXTINCTION

Daniel Principle One

1. Sinclair B. Ferguson, Lloyd J. Ogilvie, ed., *Mastering the Old Testament, Volume 19: Daniel* (Dallas: Word Publishing, 1988), 19:36.

2. Robert J. Lifton, quoted in Julia Layton, "How Brainwashing Works," *How Stuff Works*, http://science.howstuffworks.com/life/inside-the-mind/human-brain/brainwashing.

3. Charles Swindoll, *Daniel: God's Pattern for the Future* (Nashville: W Publishing, 1985), 13.

4. Ferguson, 19:19.

5. Warren W. Wiersbe, *The Bible Exposition Commentary: Old Testament* (Colorado Springs: Chariot Victor Publishing, 2002), 254.

6. Ferguson, 19:38.

7. Ibid, 19:36.

8. Ken Collier, "4 Stabilizing Truths," (Brevard, NC: The Wilds Christian Camp and Conference Center, n.d.).

9. Ideas for "The Spiritual POW Survival Guide" were patterned after the SERE program used by both Navy and Army SERE Programs (i.e., Survival Evasion Resistance Escape) during and after Operation Desert Storm.

Daniel Principle Two

1. Colin Brown, *Dictionary of New Testament Theology*, (Grand Rapids: Zondervan, 1976), 1:527.

2. R. Laird Harris, Gleason L. Archer, and Bruce K. Waltke, *Theologicial Wordbook of the Old Testament* (Chicago: Moody, 1980), 2:905.

Daniel Principle Three

1. Swindoll, 37.

2. Andrew Tuplin, "Virtual Morality," *Adbusters,* http://www.adbusters.org/magazine/80/virtual_morality.html.

3. Warren W. Wiersbe, *Be Resolute (Daniel): Determining to Go God's Direction* (Colorado Springs: David C. Cook, 2000), 54

Daniel Principle Four

1. Swindoll, 55.

2. June Hunt, "Living Guilt Free," *Hope for the Heart*, https://www.hopefortheheart.org/guilt/.

3. John MacArthur, *Daniel: God's Control over Rulers and Nations* (Nashville: Thomas Nelson, 2000), 51

PART THREE—FOURTEEN LAWS OF COURAGEOUS LEADERSHIP

Number One—The Law of Purposeful Purity

1. William Hendriksen and Simon J. Kistemaker, *New Testament Commentary* (Grand Rapids, Baker Books, 1953–2001), Biblesoft.

2. Ibid.

Number Three—The Law of Excellence

1. Hendriksen, Biblesoft.

Number Five—The Law of Sincerity

1. Mac Lynch, "The Holy Place" (Brevard, NC: The Wilds, Inc., 1989).

2. Ron Hamilton, "My Quiet Time" (Greenville, SC: Majesty Music, Inc., 1985).

Number Nine—The Law of Thankfulness

1. William A. Ward, quoted in "20 Quotes to Inspire Gratitude," http://www.habitsforwellbeing.com/20-quotes-to-inspire-gratitude/.

2. Robert Brault, quoted in "20 Quotes to Inspire Gratitude," http://www.habitsforwellbeing.com/20-quotes-to-inspire-gratitude/.

3. Aldous Huxley, quoted in "Aldous Huxley – Quotes," http://www.egs.edu/library/aldous-huxley/quotes/.

4. William A. Ward, quoted in "Wisdom Quotes," http://www.wisdomquotes.com/quote/william-arthur-ward-4.html.

Number Thirteen—The Law of Faith

1. John G. Butler, *The Analytical Bible Expositor* (Clinton, IA: LBC Publications, 2010), PC Study Bible.

2. Ibid.

3. Ibid.